Resilient Classrooms

The Guilford Practical Intervention in the Schools Series

Kenneth W. Merrell, Series Editor

Helping Students Overcome Depression and Anxiety: A Practical Guide
Kenneth W. Merrell

Emotional and Behavioral Problems of Young Children:
Effective Interventions in the Preschool and Kindergarten Years
Gretchen A. Gimpel and Melissa L. Holland

Conducting School-Based Functional Behavioral Assessments:
A Practitioner's Guide
T. Steuart Watson and Mark W. Steege

Executive Skills in Children and Adolescents: A Practical Guide
to Assessment and Intervention
Peg Dawson and Richard Guare

Responding to Problem Behavior in Schools:
The Behavior Education Program
Deanne A. Crone, Robert H. Horner, and Leanne S. Hawken

Resilient Classrooms: Creating Healthy Environments for Learning
Beth Doll, Steven Zucker, and Katherine Brehm

Resilient Classrooms

Creating Healthy Environments for Learning

BETH DOLL
STEVEN ZUCKER
KATHERINE BREHM

THE GUILFORD PRESS
New York London

A Division of Guilford Publications, Inc.
72 Spring Street, New York, NY 10012
www.guilford.com

Printed in Canada

This book is printed on acid-free paper.

Last digit is print number: 9 8 7 6 5 4 3 2

Library of Congress Cataloging-in-Publication Data

Doll, Beth, 1952–
Resilient classrooms : creating healthy environments for learning / Beth Doll, Steven Zucker, Katherine Brehm.
p. cm. — (The Guilford practical intervention in the schools series)
Includes bibliographical references (p.) and index.
ISBN 1-59385-001-8 (pbk. : alk. paper)
1. Children with social disabilities—Education—United States. 2. Children with mental disabilities—Education—United States. 3. Classroom environment—United States. I. Zucker, Steven. II. Brehm, Katherine. III. Title. IV. Series.
LC4091.D65 2004
371.9—dc22 2003025835

About the Authors

Beth Doll, PhD, is professor and director of the school psychology program at the University of Nebraska–Lincoln. She has directed several training grants preparing teachers and school psychologists to support the success of students with disabilities in regular classrooms. Her research addresses models of school mental health that enhance the well-being of students in naturally occurring communities, and program evaluation strategies that demonstrate the impact of school mental health services.

Steven Zucker, PhD, is assistant professor and coordinator of the school psychology program at the University of Colorado at Denver. As a practicing school psychologist, he developed a noncategorical service-delivery model that allowed at-risk students to receive support services without disability labels. His current research explores the efficacy of classroom-based interventions that foster academic and social competence.

Katherine Brehm, PhD, is associate professor of school psychology in the Department of Educational Psychology and Special Services at the University of Texas at El Paso. A practicing school psychologist for 15 years, her research interests include consultation and contextual intervention to support emotionally and academically successful students in culturally diverse classrooms.

Acknowledgments

This book would not have happened without the assistance and participation of teachers and students at Adams City Middle School, Arrowhead Elementary, Belmont Elementary, Castro Elementary, Gust Elementary, and West Lincoln Elementary schools in Colorado and Nebraska. We also extend our sincere appreciation to the graduate students at the University of Colorado at Denver and the University of Nebraska–Lincoln, whose contributions to our work have greatly enriched the examples and illustrations included in the book. Finally, we offer special thanks to our spouses, Bruce, Kathy, and Russ, for supporting us in our work and our partnership. After long work sessions in Lincoln, Bruce would shuttle us to the local blues club for much needed R&R. Kathy nourished us through long, hot days of working in Denver, and Russ displayed his typical patience, grace, and hospitality during our El Paso meetings. Thank you for fostering our resilience to finish this book!

Contents

1

Introduction to the Resilient Classroom

Resilient children are children who are successful despite the odds. Although they live their early years under harsh circumstances of deprivation, maltreatment, illness, or neglect, resilient children create successful lives for themselves. They earn advanced educational degrees, achieve successful careers, become financially stable, form happy and healthy families, and give back to their communities. Legends of resilient children are part of the fabric of American folklore. In fairy tales, Cinderella became a princess and lived happily ever after despite enduring years of her stepmother's abuse. The Horatio Alger novels inspired late-19th-century immigrants with rags-to-riches tales of impoverished youths who became wealthy entrepreneurs through diligence and hard work. A belief in personal resilience is captured in the common speech of our grandmothers, who spoke of "pulling yourself up by your own bootstraps."

Developmental research on risk and resilience shows that such "bootstrap" legends are largely fictional. It is true that substantial numbers of chronically deprived children are successful despite the odds, but not because they single-handedly overcome risk. Instead, truly resilient children are vulnerable children who benefited from the caring, sustenance, and guidance of a community. In Emmy E. Werner's classic study of developmental disabilities, the children who overcame high-risk childhoods were those who had a close bond with at least one caretaker, or had access to nurturing from other adults (Werner & Smith, 1982, 1992). Michael Rutter's study of the Isle of Wight showed that high-risk children were less likely to develop mental illness when they had effective parenting and positive adult models (Rutter, 1985, 1987). These resilient children had a committed and caring community pulling them upward into well-adjusted adulthood. In effect, it was the "child-in-community" that was resilient and not the child alone.

The premise of this book is that school classrooms can become resilient communities that provide essential support and guidance so that vulnerable children can learn and be successful. By drawing upon exemplary research in education, child development, and psychology, we describe the characteristics of classrooms that comprise resilience. We explain why embedding these supports into resilient classrooms is essential to every school's mission of academic excellence. Finally, we describe practical and simple-to-use strategies that can infuse resilience into the fabric of classrooms' everyday routines and practices. Our ultimate goal is to reshape current understanding of the interface between schooling and children's mental health, and to rethink existing strategies for supporting the social, emotional, and intellectual needs of high-risk children in schools.

WHY CHANGE CLASSROOMS INSTEAD OF KIDS?

North American schools are reeling under the pressures of meeting rising standards for academic excellence while educating large numbers of high-risk children. Of the 49 million children being educated in today's schools, 17% are living under conditions of abject poverty with the very real possibility that their family will not be able to pay the next month's rent or heat bills (Children's Defense Fund, 2002). Each year, 836,000 children are identified as physically or emotionally abused or neglected, and for 581,000 children the abuse is so harmful that the children are removed from their families and placed into foster care. One out of every five or six children meets the diagnostic criteria for at least one mental illness listed in the text revision of the fourth edition of the *Diagnostic and Statistical Manual of Mental Disorders* (DSM-IV-TR; American Psychiatric Association, 2000; U.S. Department of Health and Human Services, 1999). Given these prevalence rates, the typical school classroom with 25 students is likely to have at least 5 children with significant mental health needs, 4 students living in poverty, and 1 child struggling with severe abuse. Schools located in communities of concentrated poverty, unemployment, crime, and violence will inevitably show even higher rates.

Traditional models would address these needs with "change-the-kid" strategies: referring needy children into individual and group mental health services where the children learn to overcome their hardships through new understandings, improved social skills, and strengthened self-management strategies. Developmental risk research raises questions about whether these traditional strategies can be effective in changing the developmental trajectories of high-risk children (Coie et al., 1993; Doll & Lyon, 1998; Pianta, 2001b). Even more important, national statistics show that most high-risk children are not served by community mental health or social service agencies (U.S. Department of Health and Human Services, 1999). Nationwide, there is a documented gap of 12–15% of school-age children who have urgent needs for social and emotional support but are not receiving it through community providers. Schools cannot hire enough school mental health professionals to meet the needs of these children in change-the-kid ways. Instead, this gap requires that schools find other ways to support the social and emotional needs of high-risk children so that they can learn and be successful despite their risk. A premise of this book is that alternative strategies will be more enduring and most successful when they are integrated into naturally occurring systems of support that surround children.

Blueprints for designing natural supports can be found in existing research on risk, resilience, and effective schools. Longitudinal studies have shown that when high-risk children develop competence in the midst of adversity, it is because systems have operated to protect the child and counteract threats to development. Characteristic of these systems are close and nurturing relationships between children and caretaking adults, access to successful adult models, support for children's self-efficacy and achievement orientation, opportunities for children to practice self-regulation, support for warm and effective peer relationships, and "connectedness" within and among families and with formal and informal community groups that serve families (Doll & Lyon, 1998; Coie et al., 1993). Similarly, James P. Comer's experience with impoverished inner-city schools taught him that the children need caring adults to support them and school environments that support the total development of the child (Comer, Haynes, Joyner, & Ben-Avie, 1996). Emory L. Cowen, initiator of the Primary Mental Health Project, describes specific features of mentally healthy school environments: supporting secure attachments to adults, providing the child with age-appropriate competencies, exposing the child to contexts that enhance wellness, empowering the child, and preparing the child to cope effectively with stress (Cowen, 1994; Cowen et al., 1996).

Both Comer and Cowen have demonstrated success in raising the achievement of high-risk children by changing the social context of schooling. Still, these programs emphasize buildingwide infrastructures that support effective practices. This book shifts that emphasis to the immediate classroom contexts where children spend much of their school day. Complex interactions between children and their classroom environments can maximize or diminish each child's success (Pianta, 2001b; Sameroff, 1975). Thus, learning problems do not "reside" within the children but instead reflect a mismatch between the children and one or more of the features within their classrooms (Pianta & Walsh, 1996).

HOW CAN CLASSROOMS BE CHANGED?

A framework for fostering classroom change can be found in the ecological systems perspective on human development. This perspective describes each child as part of an integrated ecological system—the "child-in-classroom" (Bronfenbrenner, 1979;

Capra, 1996). Obvious features of the ecosystem of any classroom include the teacher, students, and physical setting. In this book, we also include less apparent features of the ecosystem such as the families that students come from each morning and return to at the end of each school day; the surrounding school with its policies, routines, and practices; and the community within which the school resides.

Systems perspectives explain that classroom systems change through coordinated efforts of the teacher, students, parents, and others who are part of the classroom or visit it regularly. Neither the child nor the classroom can change without changing the other. When the changes made by the teachers, parents, and students complement and support each other, that change can persist and have an enduring impact on the routines and practices of the classroom (Pianta & Walsh, 1996). Uncoordinated changes, such as those unilaterally imposed by teachers or other members of the system working in isolation, are likely to have unanticipated and unintended consequences for other aspects of the system. When this occurs, tension within the system draws it back into its former state and the change effort will have failed.

Consider the example of Lewis, a fourth grader with life-threatening asthma whose class was located in an open classroom "suite" alongside three other classrooms. Lewis's potent asthma medication left him distractible, inattentive, and disorganized. His daily seatwork was rarely completed and, despite his high intelligence, he was assigned to the slower-paced groups for work in reading and mathematics. Lewis's teacher sat him near her desk, apart from his classmates, so that he wouldn't interrupt their work. In response, Lewis spent more time daydreaming and forgot even more of his work. The school nurse decided that his inattention was asthma related and established a reinforcement program so he would remember to come to the office twice a day for his medication and treatments. The program worked for 3 weeks, and then Lewis slipped back into forgetting. By the end of the year, Lewis had a reputation for being an intractable student who wouldn't cooperate with staff efforts to help him.

Then, in his fifth-grade year, Lewis was assigned to a very different classroom. The class was organized around precise management routines. At predictable times each day, students would write assignments into their notebooks and take note of those that they had not yet completed. Seatwork instructions were always written in a standard location on one of the class blackboards. Students were taught standard routines for frequent class activities such as taking a quiz, writing an essay, or checking a math paper. Class problem-solving meetings were used to develop planned activities during class recess periods, and problems were debriefed afterward. Desks were arranged in groups of four with ample space between every group. Students described their classroom teachers as "tough but cool." By October, it was clear that Lewis was no longer a problem student. His work was usually complete and on time, he remembered to go to the office for his medicine, and class visitors noted that he was usually engaged and on task. School lounge talk suggested that Lewis had finally matured—the extra growth over the summer months had "fixed" his distractibility and inattention. We pose another alternative: that the new class routines and relationships created a context that allowed Lewis to express his competence.

How can classrooms provide effective contexts for learning? Educators need to become a catalyst for coordinated change that advances the learning goals of classrooms. This requires that they (1) understand what makes a classroom a healthy place to learn, (2) recognize when essential supports are missing in a classroom, (3) intervene to reinstate those supports when necessary, and (4) demonstrate that their interventions have enhanced the learning and development of children in the classrooms. Reinstating supports requires knowing how to foster the planning and action required to engage all essential members of the classroom in coordinated efforts to change the classroom ecology.

In this book, we apply a tested model for coordinated planning from the behavioral consultation research to the problem of ecological classroom change. Research has shown that effective behavior change occurs when there is a clear description of the problem, an identified goal for change, the collection of data before, during, and after the intervention, and a written plan for intervention (Telzrow, McNamara, & Hollinger, 2000). As this model is applied to classroom change, ecological classroom interventions will be more effective when there is:

- A precise description of any missing support that is specific, observable, and measurable.
- Baseline data that describe classroom supports before intervention.
- A goal for improvement that is specific and measurable.
- A hypothesis about why some resilience characteristics are deficient.
- A step-by-step intervention plan that describes what will be done, when, and by whom.
- Evidence that the intervention is implemented according to the plan.
- Data on classroom changes that occur in response to the intervention.
- Comparison of pre- and postintervention data to assess the intervention's impact.

HOW WILL THIS BOOK HELP?

This book aims to prepare school psychologists, school counselors, school social workers, and other educators to be catalysts for creating resilient classrooms that support academic success for all students. Toward this goal, Chapters 2, 3, and 4 draw upon existing developmental and educational research to describe resilient classrooms, including classroom characteristics that support optimal conditions for learning and the classroom practices and activities that support the features in classrooms. Chapter 5 describes ways to assess these elements of resilient classrooms. We emphasize assessment strategies that are brief, practical, and can be used repeatedly in order to track changes over time. Chapters 6, 7, and 8 describe intervention strategies, including ways to convene a classroom system for coordinated planning, strategies for including the classroom's students in change, and ways to find and implement intervention practices. Chapter 9 describes evaluation procedures that can demonstrate the effectiveness of classroom change practices. Finally, Chapter 10 describes the integration of these change-the-classroom strategies into existing school mental health services that emphasize change-the-kid strategies.

2

What Are Resilient Classrooms?

Resilient classrooms are places where all children can be successful emotionally, academically, and socially. The essential environmental supports that promote children's success have already been isolated and described in three important lines of research: developmental research that predicts risk and resilience in vulnerable children, educational research that identifies the underpinnings of academic success in high-risk urban children, and special education research that describes conditions for the successful inclusion of children with disabilities in general education classrooms. Although all three lines of research grew from different purposes, their findings identify highly similar characteristics as predicting the developmental competence of children.

Our working definition of resilient classrooms will borrow most heavily from the major studies of developmental risk that were initiated in the 1940s and 1950s, and reached maturity in the 1980s and 1990s. These longitudinal studies were carefully designed, methodologically sound, and were replicated across six or more independent research groups, so their cumulative results are very convincing. In each study, a community's children were tracked across the decades to identify the family, community, and child characteristics that predicted important life outcomes such as the children's educational achievement, employment, financial independence, and social adjustment. Results of these studies were highly consistent in identifying a small list of risk and resilience factors that ultimately predicted life outcomes (Coie et al., 1993; Doll & Lyon, 1998; Masten & Coatsworth, 1998; Masten, 2001). A striking finding of the studies is that many of the most powerful predictors were not characteristics of the children but instead described the families and communities in which the children were raised. It was this very important finding that led us to suggest that resilience should be conceptualized as a property of caretaking settings rather than of individual children (Doll & Lyon, 1998).

Children living in impoverished urban communities present a special challenge to schools because they exist within "niches of high risk" (Pianta & Walsh, 1996). In addition to poverty, these children struggle to grow up while experiencing high rates of community violence, family discord, and diminished health care—many of the factors that predict poor life outcomes. Several prominent programs have emerged to address the extensive needs of these children. Inevitably, the successful programs have emphasized strengthening personal relationships among members of the community, families, and the school. The School Development Program (Comer, Haynes, & Joyner, 1996) emphasizes the need for congruence between home and school values and expectations for children. The cornerstone of the program is a community–school team that strengthens the relationships between students and staff and between staff and parents. The ultimate purpose of the program is to give adults in the school a predictable and caring presence with the children. Similarly, the Primary Mental Health Project (Cowen et al., 1996) optimizes the success of schools by assigning nonprofessional child associates to establish a caring, trusting, and predictable relationship with young children who are at risk for school failure. The "Success for All" schools (Slavin & Madden, 2001) implement an enriched and strengthened reading curriculum, accompanied by family support teams to significantly increase family involvement in their children's education. All three programs monitor the progress of the schools by continuously collecting data that is reviewed regularly by school staff.

One out of every eight children attending public school in this country has been identified with a disability. Sadly, the education of children with disabilities has not been as successful as that of their nondisabled peers. They drop out of schools twice as often as their peers, enter into higher education at half the rate, and are far less likely to be employed after graduation (President's Commission on Excellence in Special Education, 2002). Recent efforts to strengthen results for children with disabilities have emphasized learning conditions in the general education classrooms, since most children with disabilities spend 80% of their school day in such regular education classrooms (U.S. Department of Education, 1999). Special education research has sought to identify the general education conditions that raise the educational achievements of children with disabilities. For example, the social integration of children with disabilities is stronger when peers are academically and personally supportive of each other (Brinker & Thorpe, 1986) and when the social environment supports frequent peer interactions (Johnson, Johnson, & Anderson, 1983; Salisbury, Gallucci, Palombaro, & Peck, 1995). Learning is enhanced when classmates support, help, and befriend the students with disabilities (Johnson et al., 1983). Students are more engaged in the classroom's learning activities when they are provided with one-to-one, small-group, and independent work arrangements (Logan, Bakeman, & Keefe, 1997).

From these three bodies of research, we have identified six characteristics that describe the classrooms where children can be more successful academically and interpersonally. These characteristics describe classrooms where (1) students are able to see themselves as competent and effective learners (academic efficacy), (2) students set and work toward self-selected learning goals (academic self-determination), (3) students behave appropriately and adaptively with a minimum of adult supervision (behavioral self-control), (4) there are caring and authentic relationships between teachers and the students (teacher–student relationships), (5) students have ongoing and rewarding friendships with their classmates (peer relationships), and (6) families know about and strengthen the learning that occurs in the classroom (home–school relationships). Throughout the remainder of this book, we use these six characteristics as a working definition of resilient classrooms.

In traditional models of academic success, these characteristics are frequently understood as those of individual children. For example, Martha might be seen as having great academic efficacy because of the confidence she shows in her schoolwork, while Melita is seen as having a problem with academic efficacy because she gives up too soon and will not attempt difficult work. From our ecological review of the research, we find evidence that classwide routines and practices hold great influence over the emergence of these characteristics in a classroom's students. For example, encouraging words, sensitively delivered assistance, and celebrations of success can enhance the academic efficacy of Melita, Martha, and all of their classmates. Moreover, systemic classroom characteristics are amenable to change and can do much to enhance the learning of all students who spend 30 hours per week learning together.

This chapter clearly defines each characteristic of resilient classrooms and will describe an empirical knowledge base that links each characteristic to enhanced academic engagement, improved academic performance, lower student dropout rates, and more successful inclusion of students with disabilities in regular education classrooms. Chapters 3 and 4 provide expanded explanations of each characteristic, including an explanation of what strengthens each characteristic of classroom environments, how and why each strengthened characteristic fosters children's competence, and the classroom practices and routines that support the characteristic.

ACADEMIC EFFICACY

Academic efficacy describes the beliefs that students hold about their ability to learn and be successful in the classroom. It is a construct of self-fulfilling prophecies: children who expect to be successful take steps that make their success likely, whereas those who expect to fail behave in ways that almost ensure their failure (Bandura, 1986). Empirical research has made it very clear that efficacy beliefs are specific to a task. For example, the same person might have very good efficacy for writing a book and very poor efficacy for skiing or public speaking. In the same way, academic efficacy will be different for different academic subjects. For example, some students might expect to be successful in mathematics but to fail in reading or writing. Students' academic efficacy influences such achievement behaviors as their persistence, the amount of effort they spend on learning, their efforts to organize academic learning tasks, their willingness to attempt difficult learning tasks, and whether or not they act in ways necessary to be successful (Patrick, Hicks, & Ryan, 1997; Schunk, 1989a, 1991).

In a classroom, academic efficacy emerges out of opportunities to tackle challenging learning tasks with the instructional supports that make success likely (Bandura, 1986). It is also enhanced when students see that other students like themselves are successful in learning similar tasks. Perhaps most important, it is strengthened by early, persuasive feedback from the teacher and classmates that all students can be successful. In resilient classrooms, students' successes are immediately apparent and provide occasions for mutual celebration and congratulations. For example, in a second-grade classroom, students struggled mightily with timed mathematics computation tests that were administered twice a week to satisfy district mandates. Their teacher noted that the students' math skills were stronger than their test performance suggested. Through a classwide student survey and a classroom meeting, the students explained that they could not do the tests well, expected to fail, and many suspected that their classmates were more capable than they were. To raise their likelihood of success, the teacher led the students through brief relaxation exercises before each of the timed tests. Next, the class helped her identify test-taking tricks that they could use to improve their performance. Finally, so that they noticed their own success, she graphed the classroom's overall performance and led celebrations of their successful progress.

What is the impact of academic efficacy on learning? Repeatedly, research has shown that children with higher academic efficacy earn higher grades, perform better on tests and other assignments, and progress more successfully through school (Pajares & Johnson, 1996; Pintrich & DeGroot, 1990). Studies examining the specific mechanisms of academic efficacy have shown that children with high academic efficacy complete more of their work, are more strategic in their learning, and are slower to give up on difficult work than children with low academic efficacy. More important, Schunk and Zimmerman (1997) have shown that students can be trained to be to be more efficacious and their achievement improves as a result.

BEHAVIORAL SELF-CONTROL

Classroom behaviors that are essential for learning include being responsive to the teacher and the lesson, staying actively engaged in academic work, interacting effectively with peers, and moving efficiently through transitions from one learning activity to the next (Reynolds & Kamphaus, 1992). Negative behaviors that preclude learning include fidgeting or moving about, being inattentive to the teacher or the lesson, making noises out of turn, or being aggressive or disruptive toward classmates. Innumerable studies have shown that teachers can control students' classroom behaviors by carefully managing classroom routines, supervising carefully, and systematically manipulating antecedents and consequences (Good & Brophy, 1987; Kounin, 1970;

Walker, 1995). Still, when strict behavioral contingencies are teacher imposed and teacher enforced, students may not control their own behavior outside the presence of the adults who notice and cue it (Cole & Bambara, 1992; Kazdin, 1975). A classroom demonstrates behavioral self-control when its students' behavior is appropriate for learning regardless of the presence of an authority in the room.

Problems with behavioral self-control were exemplified by a second-grade classroom, where the morning reading instruction was interrupted constantly by loud arguments among those students who were completing seatwork at their desks. The arguments erupted several times a morning and often became so loud that the teacher had to leave his reading group to resolve the conflicts. The interruptions were frustrating for the teacher, and the students worried about the hurtful arguments and were hesitant to play together at recess. To resolve the problem, the teacher and his class agreed upon a few simple rules for resolving arguments without the teacher's help. Next, the class practiced the rules during several class role plays. Finally, the class tracked their progress and awarded themselves "Friday popcorn parties" for reduced arguments. This guided practice in self-control was sufficient to reduce the classroom interruptions from 21 per day to an average of 3 per day.

When a classroom's conduct is more appropriate for learning, children's academic performance improves (Stevens, Blackhurst, & Slaton, 1991; Narayan, Heward, Gardner, Courson, & Omness, 1990; Charlop, Burgio, Iwata, & Ivancic, 1988). In part, this is because improved behavior in a classroom increases the time allocated for instruction (Gettinger, 1986), and when academic engaged time increases, learning improves (Berliner, 1988). When a classroom's students are taught to monitor their own behavior and to make decisions about whether and how to behave appropriately, it can significantly increase their academic progress (Cole, 1992; Cole & Bambara, 1992; Lazarus, 1993).

ACADEMIC SELF-DETERMINATION

Students are self-determined when they have personal goals for their own learning, can identify and solve problems that might block their achievement of those goals, and systematically select and implement actions that allow them to progress toward their goals (Wehmeyer & Metzler, 1995). Self-determined learners identify with the importance of academic learning and regulate the ways that they spend their time and the effort given to learning (Grolnick, Kurowski, & Gurland, 1999; Masten, 2001; Masten et al., 1999; Pintrich, Roeser, & DeGroot, 1994). Because they consider learning to be their own responsibility, they take credit for their successes and react to temporary failures with revised goals, new action plans, or strengthened strategies for improvement.

Resilient classrooms foster academic self-determination by giving students practice, feedback, and direct instruction in academic goal setting, decision making, problem solving, and self-evaluation of academic skills. As an example, an eighth-grade math teacher was concerned that his students lacked the self-determination that they needed to meet the state's standards for eighth-grade math. Although they seemed unaware of the fact, if the students failed one or more of the standards at the end of the year, they would not be allowed to graduate into high school math classes. To increase his students' commitment to achieving the state standards, the teacher posted a large graph on the front bulletin board and marked successes for each student as each standard was passed. Next, he delivered an instructional unit on goal setting and decision making to the class, emphasizing the overall class goal for all students to pass the standards by year's end. Students set individual goals for personal activities they would carry out in order to increase their success on the math standards tests. The class conducted weekly updates when students would mark their progress in meeting their personal goals and when the class would assess its progress toward meeting the class goal. With this kind of support for goal-directed behaviors, the students' performance on state standards tests improved markedly.

Research has consistently shown that self-determined learners are more curious, prefer more challenging tasks, independently seek to master new skills, see themselves as more competent, and have higher self-efficacy (Deci & Ryan, 1985; Deci, Hodges, Pierson, & Tomassone, 1992; Pintrich et al., 1994). Moreover, students perform better and show more academic persistence when they are working toward instructional goals that they value (Harackiewicz, Manderlink, & Sansone, 1992; Meece & Courtney, 1992). Ultimately, increased student self-determination is positively related to quality engagement in learning activities, higher levels of conceptual learning, and increased retention of learned knowledge (Ames, 1992a, 1992b).

EFFECTIVE TEACHER–STUDENT RELATIONSHIPS

Teacher–student relationships are most effective when they are warm, engaged, responsive, characterized by high demands and high expectations, and provide the class with structure and clear limits (Pianta, 1999). Still, the complexity of effective teacher–student relationships is difficult to capture in lists like these. Teacher–student relationships are also emotion-based experiences that emerge out of the teachers' ongoing interactions with their students. Modern teachers are simultaneously interacting with all the children in their class, limiting the interpersonal intimacy they can achieve with any one student and imposing some distance and stereotypy into teacher–student relationships. Pianta has shown that higher numbers of students in a class lead to fewer and less positive teacher responses to each student. Moreover, the number of students makes it more challenging for teachers to accommodate to children who are exceptional in any important respect.

In a classroom, teacher–student relationships contribute to learning by raising or lowering the students' expectations of success, reassuring them in the face of failure, and engaging them in active interaction with new knowledge. Teachers hold the larger responsibility but not the sole responsibility for forging instructional relationships that enhance the learning of their students. Students also share some power over the quality of the relationship and its expression. Indeed, while any one student's relational power is small relative to that of the teacher, the cumulative relational power of all students in a classroom can be overwhelming, especially for beginning teachers. Consider the example of an elementary choir teacher. One group of fifth graders thought that he was arrogant and condescending and found his class activities to be boring. Consequently, whenever they were required to assemble on the classroom's risers to sing, several of the boys surreptitiously used their watch crystals to dance sunbeams across the teacher's balding head. The rest of the class had trouble controlling their giggles, and the teacher frequently complained that for some reason this fifth grade was his most frustrating class to teach. Once the class became caught in this routine, the teacher could not single-handedly repair his relationship with the fifth graders.

Caring relationships among students, teachers, and other adults in a school are consistently associated with increased academic engagement and student satisfaction with school (Chaskin & Rauner, 1995). Caring teachers raise academic efficacy even in classrooms where students work in active competition with one another (Ryan, Gheen, & Midgley, 1998). Conversely, isolation and the lack of personally meaningful relationships with teachers contribute to school failure (Elias et al., 1997; Baker, Terry, Bridger, & Winsor, 1997; Pianta & Walsh, 1996). Indeed, school dropouts repeatedly say that the main reason they leave school is that no one there really cares about them (Boyer, 1983; Higgins, 1994; Phelan, Yu, & Davidson, 1994; Stevenson & Ellsworth, 1993). Comer (1993) emphasizes the particular importance of teacher–student relationships in schools serving impoverished or minority youth, saying that schools are unlikely to touch the lives of inner-city poor children in any meaningful way unless they are able to re-create a sense of community.

EFFECTIVE PEER RELATIONSHIPS

The peer relationships that occur within school classrooms are frequently the first opportunities that children have to form relationships independent of their parents' supervision and guidance. Classroom peer relationships are effective when all children in a class have supportive peer friendships and when classmates know how to resolve conflicts with one another quickly to the satisfaction of both children and without disrupting their relationships. Of these two, conflict resolution has received greater attention because unresolved conflicts are highly disruptive to the ongoing activities of the peer group and may, in extreme cases, represent a safety hazard. Research has established that conflict is present in all normal peer relationships, but in healthy interactions most students can overlook minor conflicts and find ways to resolve all other conflicts so that friendships are maintained and the interaction can continue. The promotion of peer friendships plays an equally important role in shaping classroom interactions. Students with friends have someone to sit with on the bus, someone to play with at recess, someone to eat with at lunch, someone who chooses them for his or her team, and someone to talk with during free moments in a classroom.

Early research tended to focus on the deficits of the individual students when describing problems with peer conflicts and attributed student isolation to deficits in a student's social skills, social acceptance, or social cognition. However, classroom contexts can also be reshaped so that more students in a class are included by peers and conflicts are reduced. For example, an inner-city sixth-grade classroom struggled with high rates of recess conflicts and, because many of the disagreements escalated into physical fights, students were frequently suspended for one or more days. The teacher believed that students were stressed and frightened by the many noontime fights and wanted stricter enforcement of the school rules. However, a classroom meeting revealed that the students' biggest complaint was that recess was boring because there was so little to do. Recess was held on a large, concrete slab with four basketball hoops and little else. In response, the teachers purchased a few simple games that the students could take out with them—kick bags, sponge rubber Frisbees, checkers, and some jump ropes. The classroom's suspension rate fell noticeably as a result.

The importance of peer relationships to the development of social competence is well established in the research. Having a friend in class makes it easier for students to enjoy daily activities in the classroom, easier to ask for assistance in times of stress, and much more likely that students will receive help when they ask for it (Heller & Swindle, 1983; Ladd & Oden, 1979). Alternatively, having persistent and marked difficulties with peers is one of the most common reasons why staffing teams move students with disabilities out of general education classrooms and into self-contained programs (Hollinger, 1987; Schonert-Reichl, 1993). More recently, research has shown the pivotal role that friendships play in promoting academic success. Friends help each other with academic tasks (Schunk, 1987; Wentzel, 1991a, 1991b), shape each other's enjoyment of school and learning (Ladd & Price, 1987; Wentzel, 1991a, 1991b), and reinforce each others' commitment to being in school and doing well there (Berndt, 1999; Berndt & Das, 1987; Clark, 1991). Perhaps most important, students who are unliked in elementary school drop out of middle school at five times the rate of popular students (Barclay, 1966; Kupersmidt, Coie, & Dodge, 1990).

EFFECTIVE HOME–SCHOOL RELATIONSHIPS

Most parents are not a striking presence in their child's school, and secondary parents are the least involved in their children's school experiences (Christenson, 1995; Epstein, 1995). As a result, home–school relationships are frequently awkward and forced, and teachers struggle to work cooperatively with their students' families. Teachers informally define parent involvement as family attendance at parent–teacher conferences, school assemblies, or classroom events. However, systematic study has shown that the actions that parents take within their home may be more important for their children's success than anything that parents do in the school building (Finn, 1998). Important home actions include such things as monitoring television, providing a quiet place to study, checking homework completion, and reinforcing teacher discipline. The impact of meaningful parental involvement is especially marked when teachers tell parents what specific home activities are most likely to help their children do better in school (Hoover-Dempsey, Basler, & Burow, 1995). Up to 60% of the variance in students' school success is attributable to this home "curriculum" (Walberg, 1984).

Miscommunication between home and school was seriously limiting homework completion in a second-grade classroom. Although math homework was assigned twice each week, a third of the class failed to complete it. Most students reported that they did not talk with their parents about the homework and were not sure their parents knew what they were doing at school. Together with the teacher, they set a goal to complete their homework 100% of the time and made a new rule that their parents would sign their homework. The teacher sent a note home to their parents explaining when homework would be assigned and asking them to sign the homework check-off sheet attached to each assignment. Next, the class created a homework chart that recorded all completed homework. Finally, a classwide reinforcement was used when the class met its goal. Homework completion rates rose from an average of 70 to 89%, and students reported speaking daily with their parents about their schoolwork.

When parents stay involved in their children's education, their children earn higher grades and test scores (Comer, 1993; Fehrmann, Keith, & Reimers, 1987; Steinberg, 1996), stay in school longer (Estrada, Arsenio, Hess, & Holloway, 1987), and participate more actively in learning (Sattes, 1985). Students of involved parents have higher attendance rates and lower suspension and dropout rates (National Center for Educational Statistics, 1992; Rumberger, 1995; Sattes, 1985). Alternatively, when parents are disengaged, their children's attendance is poorer, they dropout more frequently, they are more likely to become teenage parents, and they are more likely to be adjudicated by the courts (Steinberg, 1996).

SUMMARY

These six characteristics form a two-stranded tether that binds students to their classroom community. One strand emphasizes the self-agency of the classroom's students—their autonomy, self-regulation and self-efficacy. The second strand emphasizes the caring and connected relationships among members of the classroom community. Both strands are important for creating resilient classrooms that promote student success. Their importance is not only evident in educational research but has been reinforced by the many teachers and principals who have worked with us over the past 5 years. The contribution of this book is to build upon existing research by creating precise operational definitions that organize the knowledge base and make it available for practical use in schools.

3

Relationship Characteristics of Resilient Classrooms

The relationships that characterize resilient classrooms include teacher–student relationships, or the degree to which students feel supported, respected, and valued by their teacher; peer relationships, or the degree to which students have effective and mutually satisfying relationships with classmates; and home–school relationships, or the degree to which parents and children communicate about and reinforce the work of the classroom. This chapter describes the mechanisms by which these relationships support learning and mental health, the classroom practices and activities that foster effective relationships in classrooms, and classroom examples of the relationships' positive impact.

TEACHER–STUDENT RELATIONSHIPS

Watch a 13-month-old child putting blocks atop one another. His enthusiasm will grow stronger with every attempt, successful or not. His glee and determination to master block stacking will be almost palpable. In some homes, his parents will warmly praise each of his attempts while giving him repeated congratulatory "high fives." Such parental encouragement is supporting the development of a competent child. If this child is raised in a family in which parental support is absent, the child may be on a very different life path toward self-doubt, underachievement, and discouragement. Likewise, teachers encourage their students along the path to competence, and when their support is less frequent or caring, it is easier for students to falter.

How Do Effective Teacher–Student Relationships Support Student Success?

Just as sensitive parenting promotes a child's sense of security and competence, effective teacher–student relationships promote engagement and confidence in the classroom (Koplow, 2002). Children who have secure attachments to their parents arrive at school prepared to interact comfortably with teachers. They have internalized the values and beliefs that their parents hold about the world and about them, and these beliefs, in turn, influence the students' school adaptation and their cognitive and emotional capacity to learn in the classroom (Bus & van IJzendoorn, 1995; Schorr, 1997; Pianta & Walsh, 1996; van IJzendoorn & DeRuiter, 1993).

Students who feel valued by their teachers similarly internalize the values and goals that the teachers hold for them (Noddings, 1992; Connell & Wellborn, 1991; Wentzel, 1997). Moreover, learning is more important to students when their learning is important to a teacher they care about, and they will work surprisingly hard when they feel trusted by their teacher (Noddings, 1988, 1992; Werner & Smith, 1992). Once students' engagement and motivation are enhanced, they can benefit from the carefully constructed curriculum that teachers provide (Eccles, Wigfield, Harold, & Blumenfeld, 1993; Koplow, 2002; Pianta, 1999; Wentzel, 1997). Just as parental applause can be reason enough for a child to persist at stacking blocks, a teacher's sensitive responses can motivate students to plug away at a challenging assignment.

Although the bulk of research on the significance of teacher–student relationships has focused on the elementary grades, supportive relationships are also critical when students transition to middle school (Eccles, Midgley, et al., 1993; Wentzel, 1997). While teacher–student relationships grow tenuous during adolescence (Eccles, Midgley, et al., 1993), their decline in quality during the middle school years is not inevitable. In fact, teacher relationships are more directly linked to motivation and academic achievement than are peer or parental relationships (Eccles, Midgley, et al., 1993; Wentzel, 1997).

What Are Classroom Routines and Practices That Strengthen Teacher–Student Relationships?

Teachers can create an ethos of caring in the classroom by engaging in ongoing, frequent conversations with their students. Students report that caring teachers are those who talk with them, listen to their concerns, help them with their work, and communicate fairness and nurturance. These teachers share their own experiences, and their stories instill a sense of confidence in their students (Noblit, Dwight, & McCadden, 1995; Noddings, 1992; Wentzel, 1997). They show interest in the students' daily lives and know about their celebrations and disappointments. They create a classroom environment "in which students can see that their learning, their opinions, and their concerns are taken seriously" (Developmental Studies Center, 1996, p. 3). Caring is conveyed through comments that are encouraging, provide constructive feedback, and describe the teacher's high expectations for students (Wentzel, 1997). Students become attached to teachers who remind them of the collective experiences that they have shared and who tell students that they think of them often. In effective classroom communities, students' talking with supportive teachers becomes the "currency of caring" (Noblit et al., 1995).

Teachers' sensitive responses to student-initiated conversations are also influential in determining classroom adjustment (Pianta & Walsh, 1996). It is not always possible for teachers to set aside their other responsibilities when students come to them with important comments or questions, but it is possible for teachers to reliably respond even if that response is sometimes postponed. Faber and Mazlish (1995) suggest alternative ways to respond to student comments so that they leave the conversation knowing that the teacher has understood their concern and appreciates their competence. Applying basic lessons of active listening to teaching, they recommend reflecting the students' comments, validating the students' experience, avoiding blame or criticism, and helping the students make a plan rather than suggesting solutions. The pragmatics of these conversations are also important. Students will be more open in conversations where there is comfortable eye contact and they are sitting on a level with the teacher. Some teachers use a personal moment board on which students can sign up for a 5-minute chat with the teacher. Students may discuss whatever they choose during this private time and may be more likely to share personal information in these one-on-one conversations. These opportunities show students that the things they say and experience are important to their teacher.

The most essential ingredient in forging a safe, supportive classroom environment will always be the quality and consistency of the teacher's sensitive rapport with students. Important first steps in establishing rapport are knowing the students and helping the students know one another. Familiarity can be strengthened through opportunities for students to bring in pictures, trophies, or other personal possessions and talk about the importance these personally hold for them. These kinds of activities will be especially important in helping many students feel safe enough to take risks with subsequent classroom work or with classmates on the playground.

Weekly classroom meetings are another way of helping students and teachers get to know each other and contribute to the environment of the classroom. Classroom meetings are highly versatile and can be adapted to classroom planning or decision making, problem solving of social or academic difficulties, or simply checking in with the class about what the students are learning or how they are behaving. Frequent classroom meetings can foster connections between the students and the teacher, and create the expectation that the class will routinely solve its problems in cooperative and mutually satisfying ways.

A Classroom Illustration

Mr. G was a seventh-grade teacher in a rural school district. His students were primarily Latino, and the majority came from families who were struggling financially. The standardized test scores in the school were well below the state norm, and the school had been placed on notice that test scores needed to improve. While this might cause some teachers to restrict their focus to academic content, Mr. G believed that the quality of his relationships with students needed to be his top priority. He held regular classroom meetings to discuss the quality of daily life in the classroom. He collected anonymous classroom surveys from his students to describe their collective views on the classroom relationships. The surveys suggested that Mr. G's rapport with his students was exceptionally strong. Students believed that Mr. G would always find a way to help them learn even the most difficult material. When asked what made Mr. G's their favorite class, they explained, "It's the teacher who makes the class, not the material he presents"; "The teacher sets the tone for the class and how the kids behave—that's why we work quietly in here but not in other classes"; "With teachers who have no control, we wind up teasing and not sticking up for each other"; "The kids' level of excitement is based on the level of excitement of the teacher"; "He checks in with each group individually—he doesn't just give us answers, he helps us figure it out"; "Mr. G listens to us—if we don't get it, we have a class discussion about it"; "He doesn't treat us like kids—he doesn't insult us—he listens to us"; "This is not a class, it's a democracy!" For these students, the influence of the classroom relationships on behavior was pronounced. Their social behavior and their academic engagement were far more positive in this favorite class than in their other classes.

PEER RELATIONSHIPS

Students' relationships with classroom peers are highly predictive of their academic and social engagement in classroom activities (Connell & Wellborn, 1991). Effective peer relationships create a social context in the classroom that prompts students to actively participate in learning activities, maintain interest in academic tasks, develop social competence, and be successful in learning (Malecki & Elliott, 2002; Wentzel, 1993).

How Do Effective Peer Relationships Support Student Success?

In resilient classrooms, there are norms and rules for how students interact with each other so that they have comfortable friendships and resolve conflicts efficiently and satisfactorily. These norms and rules emerge out of the shared expectations of all students and adults who work in the classroom. This creates a social context where students value and pursue the classroom's shared social and academic goals (Connell & Wellborn, 1991; Malecki & Elliott, 2002; Wentzel, 1999). When students feel like important members of their classes, they become more thoroughly engaged in the classroom's social and academic activities and learning is enhanced (Wentzel & Watkins, 2002). It is not always possible to measure the quality of these relationships through objective observations or assessments. However, student ratings are powerful measures of peer relationships because it is relationships' perceived quality, from the students' perspective, that fosters an important sense of well-being and social relatedness (Wentzel, 1999).

Prosocial behaviors such as sharing, helping, and cooperating are essential to these norms because they provide the foundation for such crucial academic processes as problem solving and academic motivation (Wentzel & Watkins, 2002). Whereas interventions that foster prosocial behaviors in the classroom frequently lead to improvements in academic performance, interventions designed to improve academic achievement do not show corresponding increases in prosocial classroom behaviors (Cobb, 1972; Cobb & Hops, 1973; Coie & Krehbiel, 1984; Hops & Cobb, 1974). The relationship is bidirectional, but the influence of prosocial behavior on achievement is far stronger than the influence of achievement on peer relationships (Wentzel, 1993). In essence, this means that educators that respond to mandates of high-stakes testing by stressing content drills in the classroom are missing an important opportunity to promote academic success through relationship building.

Still, effective peer relationships are much more than prosocial behaviors. In resilient classrooms, all students are included in multiple peer friendships with their classmates and these are the students that they eat lunch with, go to recess with, and spend time with during any unstructured classroom moments (Berndt & Perry, 1986; Buhs & Ladd, 2001). These mutual peer friendships emerge out of having fun doing things together and are maintained when students have frequent enjoyable interactions with their friends (Renshaw & Asher, 1983). In addition to caring for and sharing with one another, friends routinely joke around, tease each other, call each other names, play fight, and push and shove—jostling behaviors that mimic peer aggression but have very different intentions within the trust and intimacy of friendships (Pellegrini, 2002).

What Are Classroom Routines and Practices That Strengthen Peer Relationships?

Teachers can organize students' social interactions in classrooms so that social-developmental tasks are within the students' zone of proximal development (Pianta, 1999). For example, early elementary students are usually able to work in pairs but late elementary students can often work in slightly larger groups of four. Older students are better able to work together despite widely disparate skill levels, whereas younger students can struggle when asked to work cooperatively with students who are too different from themselves. Groups can be carefully composed so that they include some students with strong leadership abilities, others with effective conflict resolution skills, and still others capable of explaining the assigned task. In most cases, students will need explicit training in how to work collaboratively as a group, help their partners, explain their understanding, and engage all group members in the task (Wentzel & Watkins, 2002).

Classroom practices can also promote prosocial behaviors by encouraging students to share resources, work constructively together, and solve problems in a positive and productive manner (Blumenfeld, Hamilton, Wessels, & Falkner, 1979; Koplow, 2002; Sieber, 1979; Wentzel, 1993). For example, in a fourth-grade classroom, a classroom meeting to discuss frequent playground arguments prompted the students to write a comprehensive set of soccer rules for their noontime game. Chapter 5 describes a classroom where students reduced the intimidation on their playground through a program to welcome new students into their class. In both cases, classroom conflicts were significantly reduced once students proposed and implemented solutions that their teacher had not anticipated. Prosocial behaviors emerge and conflicts are diminished in classrooms where there are open discussion of students' ongoing activities, problems, and celebrations (Doll, 1996; Mulvey & Cauffman, 2001). In addition to providing valuable practice in social problem solving, classroom meetings about peer conflicts also make the varying viewpoints of classmates explicit and so provide students with direct instruction in perspective taking and empathy (Doll, 1996; Mulvey & Cauffman, 2001).

Classroom routines can also facilitate peer friendships, but it is not necessary to explicitly direct classmates' personal relationships with each other. Instead, practices can be embedded into the daily routines and rituals of classrooms that will support students' peer relationships without being overly prescriptive (Doll, 1996). Simply put, friendships emerge from frequent opportunities to have fun working and playing together. Incidental activities are as effective or more effective in fostering friendships as are activities with the explicit purpose of teaching social skills. For example, a fifth grader who was new to her school volunteered for cafeteria cleanup because students were always assigned in pairs and it gave her an opportunity to work with a potential friend. Children's opportunities for classroom friendships expand geometrically if their working groups are periodically rearranged so that they have a chance to work with less familiar classmates as well as those whom they know well. It is not enough to place students together without also providing them with enjoyable and relevant activities to do. For this reason, classroom recess periods can be missed opportunities for shaping peer relationships unless the playground has sufficient fun games to play. Boring playgrounds can create conflicts within peer groups. A sixth grader explained, "If there's not enough to do, fighting is a lot more fun than doing nothing."

Interventions to promote positive peer relationships will be most effective when applied within the classroom environment where students live and learn rather than through traditional pullout services to promote social competence (Pianta, 2001b). Children's empathy, their orientation toward interpersonal relationships, and their ability to regulate behavior are processes that develop over time in the context of frequent and satisfying interactions with peers. Within natural classroom groups, higher achieving or more socially competent classmates can be taught to coach less skilled classmates and engage them in strategic problem-solving behavior (Wentzel & Watkins, 2002). As a result, all students in a class benefit.

Students who are less socially adept can also benefit from opportunities to work or play together in pairs or very small groups with their more competent classmates. Many students have a difficult time negotiating work or play within large groups of students. Mixing in large groups is especially difficult when there are unfamiliar students from other classes, as occurs in the lunchroom and on the playground. Large groups prompt greater anxiety in students who are prone to self-isolate, making it more difficult for them to initiate interactions with classmates or secure invitations to play. Timid students are easily overlooked within the chaos and disorganization of larger peer groups. Teachers who acknowledge and discuss these challenges with students can normalize the feelings of withdrawn students, raise their classmate's awareness of their feelings, and prompt their classmates to take the first step to include them more often. "Schools need to examine ways to reengineer the social opportunities available to students so that the task of adjusting to peers is less onerous and more possible for a broader group of students" (Doll, 1996, p. 177).

A Classroom Illustration

A fifth-grade teacher was worried about her students' verbal aggression in the classroom and physical aggression on the playground. Through anonymous student surveys, she learned that the students thought the disagreements were caused by the very competitive soccer game played during each lunchtime recess. They explained that if they didn't play soccer there would be nothing else to do. As an alternative, the school psychologist offered to teach the students noncompetitive games that they could play at recess. The class planned a Frisbee course using existing playground equipment and "soft" Frisbees. They tackled group problem-solving skills using Hula-Hoop games. In the classroom, similar games were used as an appropriate reward for productive academic work. (These games are described more fully at the end of Chapter 8.) The teacher also held postrecess classroom meetings to discuss that day's play and students' efforts to be more cooperative. Six weeks later, the surveys were readministered and showed that the number of arguments and fights had decreased considerably.

HOME–SCHOOL RELATIONSHIPS

Contextual influences on students' learning and behavior extend beyond the classroom to include the home–school relationship. Just as the classroom context can influence the quality of communication that occurs among students and teachers, the classroom context can influence the understanding that develops between the class and students' families.

How Do Effective Home–School Relationships Support Student Success?

The academic orientation and instructional practices of the home exert substantial influence on students' academic competence. In particular, students' learning is supported by the pattern of home–school interactions over time (Pianta & Walsh, 1996). When these interactions are sufficiently frequent and relevant, families and schools develop shared understanding of the child'schildren's needs that allows them to convey congruent messages to the childabout learning and school.

There is enormous variability in the skills, attitudes, values, and resources that children from different families bring to school. Some students come to school from families where the educational values and expectations are quite consistent with the school. Some do not. Some students come from families that have many rich and varied resources to support learning. Some do not. While this variability presents unique challenges for schools, it is important to disentangle what parents do from what parents have. It is what parents and schools do that matters most for students' learning and social competence (Coleman & Schneider, 1993).

Students' beliefs and expectations about academic achievement are highly influenced by parental and teacher beliefs about the value of education and their expectations for the child's success (Christenson, Rounds, & Gorney, 1992; Connell & Wellborn, 1991; Jacklin, 1989; Noddings, 1992; Wentzel, 1997). When the home and the school share a relationship and communicate effectively, their educational goals and values will be more similar and students will more readily internalize this shared value (Christenson & Anderson, 2002; Pianta & Walsh, 1996). Remarkably, the convergence of home and school values about students's learning and behavior is more influential than family economic status in predicting academic success (Christenson & Godber, 2001; Christenson et al., 1992; Coleman & Schneider, 1993). The converse is also true. Students who experience significant discontinuity between their home, peer, and school worlds are most at risk for poor school performance and emotional problems (Pianta & Walsh, 1996).

Students learn best when families and classrooms hold high expectations for effort, behavior, and desired performance; clearly describe the rules and guidelines for school-related tasks; demonstrate their support for and interest in the student; and model consistency in directions, problem solving, and goal setting (Christenson & Peterson, 1998). When these practices are present in both home and school, students internalize the education-enhancing values held by parents and teachers and their achievement rises (Chall, 2000; Christenson & Peterson, 1998). As home and school efforts become more connected, their influence on a student's success is enhanced. Students gain a sense of belongingness or membership in a learning community that, in turn, is associated with positive attitudes toward school and active participation in the learning activities of the classroom (Osterman, 2000).

What Are Classroom Routines and Practices That Strengthen Home–School Relationships?

Strategies for promoting effective home–school relationships often go beyond the scope of an individual classroom to include schoolwide or districtwide programs (e.g., Christenson & Godber, 2001; Christenson & Sheridan, 2001). While these should be a top priority, our goal in this section is to detail practices that teachers can use to raise parental involvement in their own classrooms.

Parental involvement at home and parental involvement at school are not equally important to children's learning. Student achievement is influenced more by what parents do to support their children's schooling in the home than by what they do inside the school building (Finn, 1993, 1998; Sui-Chu & Willms, 1996). Frequent student–

parent conversations about school provide an indirect gauge of parents' engagement in their children's education and suggest that education is integrated into the life of the family. Teachers can facilitate this integration by initiating and maintaining open lines of communication with the home. Parents are more highly and consistently involved when they believe that their participation is directly related to the achievement of their students (Finn, 1998).

A good place to start is informing parents about effective, complementary home-based practices that support their children's work in the classroom. Research reports about parental practices that raise achievement can be reframed as classroom tips in newsletters, phone calls, or personal notes sent to parents in students' homework folders. These can let parents know how important it is for them to convey high expectations, set firm but reasonable standards around effort and performance, and enforce rules around homework routines. In bilingual or low-income communities, parents do not always understand how to do the work that their children bring home from the classroom and sometimes they believe that they cannot help their children with homework. However, parents can become cheerleaders for their students by reassuring and encouraging them, and by cultivating their children's diligence and persistence in the face of challenges (Bempechat, Graham, & Jimenez, 1999).

Students can share responsibility for fostering more communication with their parents about school. For example, students can be assigned to interview their parents and report back on their parents' knowledge of the daily routines and practices of the classroom. They can use their parents as "experts" that they consult when researching classroom topics. For example, in a unit on relationships between the United States and the Middle East, some students could interview their parents who served in the Gulf War while others could interview family members who were displaced by the war into refugee camps. Students might gather their parents' suggestions for modifying classroom practices so that they are more family-friendly or better support student learning. For example, parents might have ideas about the schedule of classroom assignments, the amount of homework support that parents should provide, or what the classroom can do to help parents help from home.

Classroom teachers' efforts to involve parents will not be successful unless such efforts are mutual. In the same way that schools recommend that parents do certain things with their children, parents should have opportunities to make recommendations to the classroom. Traditionally, teachers have asked parents to help by supervising field trips, holding bake sales, copying classroom materials, or filing library cards. Instead, the PTA Quality Indicators suggest that parents be asked for recommendations about course offerings, student course schedules and class placement, optional enrichment programs that the school may develop, or the quality of their children's schoolwork (National Parent–Teacher Association, 1997). The contrast between these lists is striking. The first list incorporates a number of menial tasks that do not respect or use the talents that parents frequently have. The second list includes the parents as full partners in planning, delivering, and evaluating their child's education. Most parents are not accustomed to being asked for these kinds of recommendations, and so teachers will need to actively solicit meaningful parental inputs (Christenson &

Sheridan, 2001). This will require that classrooms be welcoming, use a variety of communication strategies to reach all parents, adjust communications to different languages and cultural expectations, and—above all else—be responsive to parental recommendations once they are made.

The most successful efforts to encourage parental involvement in the classroom are convenient for families, clearly relevant to school success, and emphasize honest, respectful, collaborative interactions with families (Schorr, 1988, 1997). Classroom efforts to initiate these interactions are especially critical among low-income families in which students' academic achievement is highly dependent upon parental interest, support, and encouragement (Patrikakou & Weissberg, 2000; Peña, 2000).

A Classroom Illustration

In a third-grade classroom, most students were from Spanish-speaking families and their parents' limited English made it difficult for them to help with schoolwork. The teacher, the school psychologist, and the students brainstormed solutions to this dilemma and decided to show their parents how they could help. The teacher sent a letter home to parents in English and Spanish asking for permission to videotape the teacher and their child working together on typical homework problems. This alone generated more parent communication than before. The videotape was crafted so that every student in the classroom was shown for a brief segment being helped by the teacher. In this way parents had an opportunity to "meet" their child's classmates and gain a mental picture of the classroom. The parents also had a chance to see an effective teacher in action and to gain more confidence about what they could do to help their child. Students reported that they had to translate much of the dialogue on the videotape and that this prompted additional discussions about classroom practices and the nature of assignments.

SUMMARY

In this chapter we have provided a more complete description of the mechanisms by which effective classroom relationships promote students' academic and social success. For purposes of clarity, we have described the three relational characteristics of resilient classrooms in separate sections, but this separation does not sufficiently acknowledge the potentiating influences that occur when these relationships are considered in unison. For example, the quality of teacher–student relationships can influence students' social competencies and so contribute to the peer relations in a classroom and to students' academic and social risk taking. Alternatively, when parents respect their students' teachers and reinforce the teachers' rules and recommendations, students are likely to form more comfortable teacher–student relationships. All three kinds of relationships contribute to the classroom's social context for learning, fostering an environment that is emotionally comfortable, encourages risk taking, and provides the student with a sense of being valued and respected. Relational factors can also impact students' academic success by setting the stage for the promotion of self-agency characteristics. These will be discussed more fully in Chapter 4.

ONE MORE EXAMPLE: CHANGING CLASSROOM RELATIONSHIPS

Like many of the classrooms that we have worked with, this third–fourth–fifth-grade combination classroom was struggling with serious problems with recess. The fighting and arguing had become so constant and so intense that students came back into the classroom distraught and unable to work. Teachers and the special services team thought that the conflicts were mostly due to Briana, a student with serious emotionally disabilities who frequently bullied and sometimes assaulted the other students. Their first thought was to restrict Briana's recess privileges and take turns supervising her during the rest of the class's playtime. Before taking such an extreme action, the school psychologist spent a full week collecting recess reports as the class came in from the playground. Students filled out a daily checklist noting whether they had struggled with one or more of the typical recess problems: being teased, having a rotten time, losing a friend, not being allowed to join others in their play, physical fighting, arguing, or having to play alone. The results are shown graphically in Figure 3.1. The reports showed that students weren't having a lot of fun, even when no conflicts had occurred. They struggled with lots of arguing, being left out, and having to play alone.

In a follow-up meeting of the teacher with the class, the students explained that missing or broken equipment had made it impossible for them to play many recess games, so most students played "horde" soccer with two huge 25-person teams. There were no goalposts, so students tried to mark the goals with jackets and often marked five or more goal areas around the field. The crowded soccer field was ripe with fights and arguments, and with so many players the game was often boring for students on the periphery.

Now, attention of the team was refocused away from Briana and toward making more games available on the playground. The assistant principal moved the playground equipment budget out of the gym teacher's budget and used the playground funds to purchase tetherballs, kick balls, and jump ropes. Then, she worked with the local parks department to mark goal areas on the soccer field and to repaint the playground's four-square court so that it was on flat pavement rather than a sloping hill. The school psychologist purchased some playground games books and worked with a group of four or five students to identify fun games and teach them to the rest of the class. The classroom teachers helped the students research the official rules of soccer and established class procedures to select soccer teams fairly and quickly. The playground paraprofessionals worked with the school psychologist to establish tighter and more effective supervision procedures, with the ultimate goal of stopping arguments before they got worse.

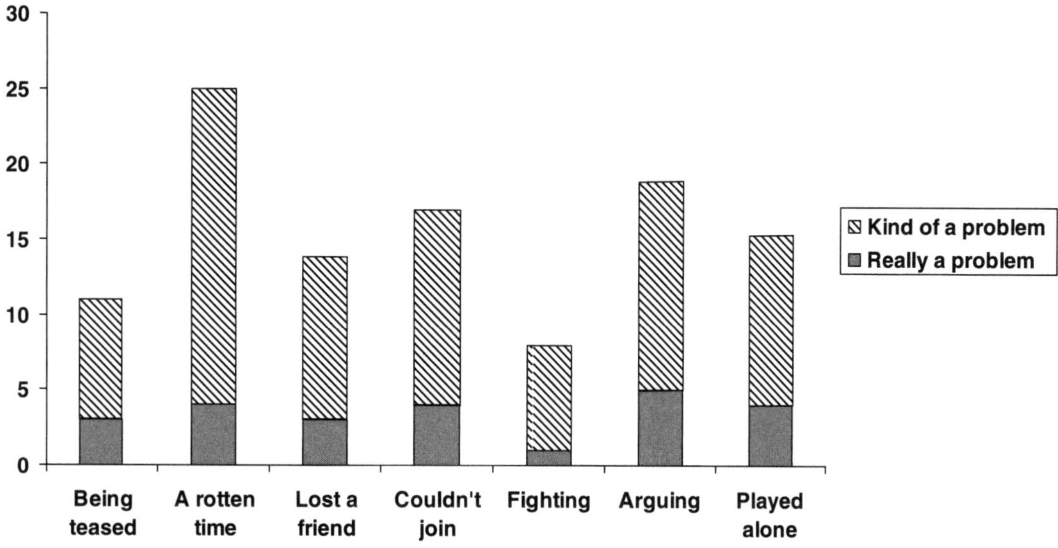

FIGURE 3.1. Percentage of recesses when these problems were reported in Brianna's classroom.

Efforts to improve recess for this class stretched across several weeks and involved the participation of adults at all levels of the school organization. Ultimately, the number of recess problems was dramatically reduced. Relationships in the classroom, among students and between the students and their teachers, were strengthened by this intervention. Fewer complaints about Brianna and fewer reports home about students' recess problems improved the quality of parent–teacher communications.

ANNOTATED BIBLIOGRAPHY

Christenson, S. L., & Anderson, A. R. (2002). Commentary: The centrality of the learning context for students' academic enabler skills. *School Psychology Review, 31,* 378–393.

Wentzel, K. R., & Watkins, D. E. (2002). Peer relationships and collaborative learning as contexts for academic enablers. *School Psychology Review, 31,* 366–377.

Part of a *School Psychology Review* miniseries on promoting academic enablers, these two articles illustrate how social and academic outcomes in school are inextricably linked to the contextual features of the learning environment. Contextual features include effective peer relationships, the quality of the home–school relationship, and community resources that provide positive role models, support high academic expectations, and provide guidance, monitoring, and supervision. The role of family–school–peer relationships on student's motivation and engagement are discussed by

Christenson and Anderson, who offer recommendations for future research. Wentzel and Watkins explore the underlying mechanisms by which peer relationships can foster a sense of social relatedness and belongingness in classrooms that supports academic success. They review classroom strategies that support effective peer relationships, student's motivation, engagement, and problem-solving skills, and their academic success.

Christenson, S. L., & Sheridan, S. M. (2001). *Schools and families: Creating essential connections for learning.* New York: Guilford Press.

This book describes how school mental health professionals can forge and sustain effective partnerships among schools and families. It sheds light on critical issues these partnerships face such as the need to respect parents', students', and teachers' rights in the educational process, and parents' and teachers' respective roles and responsibilities in promoting positive student outcomes. Strategies for creating and sustaining partnerships are reviewed, including methods for garnering administrative support, implementing family–school problem-solving teams, identifying and managing the inevitable conflicts that arise between schools and families, and strategies for improving the quality of communication among teachers and parents. The book provides useful appendices such as a checklist of quality indicators of national standards for parent/family involvement and a practical inventory to guide the creation of school–family connections.

Doll, B. (1996). Children without friends: Implications for practice and policy. *School Psychology Review, 25,* 165–183.

This review of the developmental research on children's friendships describes alternative reasons why some students in a classroom may lack friends. Contextual strategies are described that promote friendships by altering the classroom's setting, routines, or practices.

Pianta, R. C. (1999). *Enhancing relationships between children and teachers.* Washington, DC: American Psychological Association

This book articulates a relational approach to teaching and learning that integrates developmental systems theory with sensible, empirically derived intervention practices. The book explores the dynamic aspects of child–teacher relationships that influence children's adaptation and competence in the classroom. Tools and strategies for assessing these complex relationships are provided, along with practical guidance for influencing student development, teacher efficacy, and systemic policies that ameliorate risk in classrooms and schools. Consultation strategies are provided to help the school mental health professional understand, enter into, and shape teacher–child relationships in positive directions. These methods can reenergize teachers' motivation and their emotional investment in and psychological connection with their students.

Pianta, R. C., & Walsh, D. J. (1996). *High-risk children in schools: Constructing sustaining relationships.* New York: Routledge.

This text provides a systemic framework for understanding children's adaptation to school and the role that educators can play in enhancing student outcomes. Its contextual systems model views school failure as a relationship problem. The model asserts that children's success in school is enhanced when there is effective communication and shared educational values among the school, family, and community systems. Insensitive organizational structures can place undue stress on students by requiring them to negotiate relationships with numerous teachers, aides, and special education providers and adjust to frequent changes in classroom routine and structure. The solution lies less in the massive restructuring of schools than in promoting effective dialogue and common goals among educators, students, and their families.

4

Self-Agency Characteristics of Resilient Classrooms

Resilient classrooms promote self-agency by helping students feel competent to meet academic challenges (academic efficacy), take responsibility for their learning (academic self-determination), and manage their own behavior (behavioral self-control). This chapter describes the mechanisms by which academic efficacy, academic self-determination, and behavioral self-control support students' success; the classroom activities and practices that promote self-agency; and classroom examples of each characteristic's positive impact.

ACADEMIC EFFICACY

Resilient classrooms improve student achievement by strengthening students' beliefs about what they can accomplish. Students' collective beliefs about their ability to succeed in school are called academic efficacy. Academic efficacy is a primary motivator of their efforts, interest, and aspirations for learning. It gives them the confidence to take risks needed for learning. These efficacy beliefs come both from within the child and from external sources, such as an anticipated reward or the praise of a well-liked teacher. Consequently, it is disturbing that students' perception of their academic capability declines precipitously across their school career. Kindergarten children enter school with highly positive views of their abilities. By third grade, however, students begin to significantly underestimate their abilities, and by middle school this decline is dramatic (Eccles, Wigfield, et al., 1993; Paris, Byrnes, & Paris, 2001).

Students with low academic efficacy avoid difficult tasks altogether or give up easily. They do not aspire to high achievement, and their commitment to any learning goals they set is weak. They interpret failure as a sign of their low ability, causing them to lose faith in their capability. On the other hand, students with a high sense of academic efficacy interpret difficult tasks as a challenge to be mastered and increase their efforts until they are successful. A strong sense of efficacy in one skill area may transfer to similar skills, evidence that "success breeds success" (Bandura, 1997). The task for educators is to create resilient classrooms that offer support for high academic efficacy.

How Does Academic Efficacy Support Student Success?

Students' interest in an academic task or the importance they assign to it can engage them in initial attempts to learn it, somewhat like a "starter" for a car. In contrast, efficacy beliefs are important for "steering" their actual performance by focusing their efforts and maintaining their commitment to the task over time (Wolters & Pintrich, 1998). Positive efficacy beliefs exert their strongest influence by enhancing basic cognitive skills, such as memory and attention (Multon, Brown, & Lent, 1991). Students' performance on classwork improves once their memory and attention become more deliberate, and eventually these improvements will be reflected in higher scores on standardized tests. Thus, academic efficacy contributes to classroom resilience by allowing students to use skills that they already possess, and their subsequent success reaffirms their efficacy beliefs.

Once students become engaged in a difficult learning task, strong academic efficacy motivates them to participate actively, persist longer, and put more mental effort into the task (Bandura, 1997; Salomon, 1984). Students' efficacious expectations of success also enhance their use of self-regulation strategies, including such strategies as concentrating on the task, using proper procedures, managing time effectively, and seeking assistance as necessary (Zimmerman, 1994). These improvements in strategy use have been demonstrated in students of all ability levels (Bouffard-Bouchard, 1989). Finally, students with stronger academic efficacy set challenging goals for themselves and are more firmly committed to reaching those goals (Bandura, 1993; Zimmerman, Bandura, & Martinez-Pons, 1992). Clearly, the achievement of these goal-directed, efficacious students is likely to be higher than that of students who lack persistence and use less efficient strategies (Multon et al., 1991; Pajares & Miller, 1994; Zimmerman et al., 1992).

The same academic efficacy that promotes student achievement also enhances their social and emotional adjustment. Students with a strong sense of efficacy are less vulnerable in the face of failure, anxiety, stress, and depression (Bandura, 1993, 1997). For example, efficacy beliefs can reduce the effect of anxiety in academically threatening situations (Siegel, Galassi, & Ware, 1985). In states with high-stakes testing, enhanced academic efficacy can be an antidote to and a protective factor against the anxiety, stress, and depression that such testing can arouse.

Although individuals hold efficacy beliefs, academic efficacy is also a group phenomenon (Bandura, 1997). Groups such as teams of teachers, classrooms, schools, and districts develop a sense of collective efficacy characterized by Bandura (1997) as "a group's shared belief in their capabilities to realize given levels of attainment" (p. 477). The stronger the beliefs that groups hold about their collective capabilities, the more they achieve. Members of the group promote mutual efficacy by encouraging each other, and evidence of the success of any single group member reaffirms the other members' beliefs that they too can succeed. These shared beliefs can overcome such powerful influences as low socioeconomic status and a history of poor academic achievement (Bandura, 1993).

What Are Classroom Routines and Practices That Strengthen Academic Efficacy?

Academic efficacy is strengthened when students are provided with mastery experiences in which they complete moderately challenging tasks with only occasional help from others (Bandura, 1977a; Skinner, 1996). When tasks are too easy students' success holds little value for them, and when tasks are much too difficult students are reduced to watching someone else solve the tasks without them. Failure can undermine efficacy development, especially if it occurs early in the learning process before efficacy is firmly established (Bandura, 1977a). Thus, it is a disservice to assign very easy tasks to students or assist students to complete tasks that are beyond their ability to complete independently. This is not to say that students should never be given help with their work, but rather that the task difficulty should not be so high that students are entirely dependent on someone else's skill to complete the task.

A simple way to adjust task requirements to student needs is to routinely include students in decisions about what tasks should be completed and in what order, what are appropriate homework assignments, and how learning should be evaluated (Eccles, Wigfield, et al., 1993). Student choice is especially important for sustaining efficacy beliefs during the transition to middle school, because student opportunities to participate in class decision making declines significantly once they leave the elementary grades. In effect, this creates a mismatch between the young adolescents' increasing desire and growing abilities to self-direct their learning and the classroom practices that provide limited opportunities to do so.

Students may attribute their success on academic tasks to their strong efforts or to their high ability, and these attributions can affect academic efficacy differently. Young students are more likely to emphasize the role of effort when explaining their successes ("I worked really hard"), but older students place more importance on their ability to complete the task ("I'm good at this"). At any age, teachers are more credible when they give effort feedback for early successes on tasks that students are just learning, because students must realistically apply effort when first learning a skill. However, teachers should then switch to ability feedback as the skill develops, because ability attributions are more important for sustaining task performance over time (Schunk, 1989a).

Peers hold strong influence over their classmate's academic efficacy beliefs. Peer models are more effective than adult models in strengthening efficacy, especially if they demonstrate coping rather than mastery. Coping models make comments like "I'm not sure I can do this, but I'll keep trying" while working on a difficult task. In contrast, mastery models complete the task quickly and competently without voicing their doubts or strategies. The use of peer models is important because struggling students may doubt that they can attain an adults' level of competence but realistically expect to match the competence of their peers. Multiple peer models are even more effective than a single model and are an inherent resource of resilient classrooms (Schunk, 1989a). Peer models are routinely available when classroom instruction incorporates reciprocal teaching or the use of collaborative learning groups (Fantuzzo & Rohrbeck, 1992; Schunk, 1983, 1991).

While positive statements about competence can raise the efficacy of all students in a class, consistently failing students should never be told that they would be successful if only they tried (Schunk, 1989b, 1991). Students with already low academic efficacy experience further inadequacy when given this kind of feedback about their failure. Instead, struggling students need concrete evidence of small incremental gains in achievement that are tied to their own efforts (Jinks & Morgan, 1999). When students track their own progress toward learning goals, they gain more powerful and positive messages about their efficacy than when their performance is compared to that of other students (Ames, 1990; Schunk, 1989b). Highlighting and publicly celebrating the strategies that led to individual and group success provide "teachable moments" when efficacy-building behaviors can be modeled. In some cases, students need to be taught how to accept public recognition of success. In all cases, classmates must be discouraged from making negative comments about each other.

Zimmerman, Bonner, and Kovach (1996) promote academic efficacy by teaching students to compare their task success to self-monitoring notes that they keep about their use of study time and daily feelings of efficacy. Students are placed in small teams and given regular study periods during class time. During these periods, they teach each other specific skills while keeping written records of the strategies that are used, the things that they learn, and their expectations of success if they were tested over the skill that day. Then, students are guided through evaluations of the impact that their strategies and efficacy have on subsequent test performance. The systematic record keeping makes these relationships explicit for the students and makes them more aware of how they can impact their own task performance by what they believe and what they do.

A Classroom Illustration

In an eighth grade elective Spanish class, anonymous student surveys revealed that students did not feel confident that they could make good grades on weekly vocabulary tests. In response, the teacher placed the students into two-person teams and gave them 20 minutes daily to teach each other five vocabulary words from the next test. Teams were then taught several alternative strategies to use when teaching each other.

Each day, they calculated and recorded their efficacy scores for the teaching strategies that they had used, and then planned their study time for the following day. Once a week, they compared their daily notes to the actual score that they received on the Friday test. Over time, the teams came to prefer the teaching strategies that increased their efficacy and raised their test scores. The study teams allowed these students to see the relationship between their effort and efficacy and to benefit from peer group modeling.

ACADEMIC SELF-DETERMINATION

Students are self-determined when they have personal goals for their own learning, can identify and solve problems that might block their achievement of those goals, and systematically select and implement actions that allow them to progress toward their goals (Deci & Ryan, 1985; Wehmeyer & Metzler, 1995). Self-determined students are every teacher's ideal students. They understand the relevance of the things they are learning in the classroom, and they will spend the time and make the effort that it takes to be successful (Pintrich et al., 1994).

How Does Academic Self-Determination Support Student Success?

Students in resilient classrooms demonstrate self-determination through academic goal setting. Goals promote self-determination by focusing student efforts on activities that support the goals and away from goal-irrelevant activities (Locke & Latham, 2002). Goals also energize students to participate more actively in instruction because its relevance is more evident. Goals affect persistence because students will sustain their efforts when they are allowed to choose how much time they spend on a task. By setting a goal and working toward it, students seek out large amounts of unfamiliar information and strategies once they discover that it is necessary for their goal achievement.

The kinds of goals that students set have different effects on achievement. Mastery goals (sometimes called task goals) describe students' goals to understand more, acquire new knowledge, or master new skills. Extrinsic goals are goals to engage in tasks because of students' desire to gain external benefits such as rewards or privileges. Performance or relative ability goals describe students' goals to excel relative to their classmates, or at least to be seen by other people as excelling. Mastery goals have been associated with higher achievement because they prompt students to devote focused, sustained efforts to achieving the goal even if it requires that they give up free time or other activities that they enjoy. Performance and extrinsic goals can be detrimental to independent learning because they make students dependent upon other people's standards for their learning and on the incentives that other people offer (Ames, 1992a, 1992b; Dweck & Leggett, 1988; Pintrich & Schunk, 1996). However, recent research indicates that students who both want to do better than others (performance goals) and want to learn and understand the material (mastery goals) show similar motivational patterns as students who have only mastery goals (Pintrich, 2000). Pintrich concludes that the competition and social comparison that typically occurs in classrooms may not have detrimental effects if classrooms are also structured to promote mastery goals.

Goals can also be defined according to their specificity, difficulty level, and proximity (Bandura, 1977b). Each of these dimensions contributes to the effectiveness of a goal. Goals that incorporate specific performance standards (e.g., the number of math problems to be completed) are more likely to lead to task success than nonspecific goals like "Do your best." Short-term or proximal goals ("Turn in the first 25 math problems tomorrow") lead to higher performance and quicker success than long-term goals ("I'll raise my math grade one letter by the next report card"). Finally, challenging but attainable goals increase motivation better than do goals that appear too easy or too difficult (Schunk, 1991).

Poor academic goals and discouraging beliefs about their own cognitive competence can combine to keep students from asking for help when they need it. Adolescents were more likely to feel threatened by the thought of asking for help when they thought they were less capable of doing the classwork, and when they were only doing the work because of adult expectations and consequences (A. M. Ryan & Pintrich, 1997). On the other hand, students with mastery goals were more likely to ask for help because doing so gave them additional control over the task and their ultimate success.

In classrooms where external deadlines and rewards are used to pressure students to work harder, these actually undermine students' self-determination (Adelman & Taylor, 1990). Conversely, students will be autonomously motivated to do classwork if they help determine their own rewards for success and set their own task deadlines (Deci, Nezlek, & Sheinman, 1981). Moreover, students who are autonomously motivated remember what they learn better than those who are motivated by external benefits or threats (Grolnick & Ryan, 1987). For example, when students were asked to learn material for a test (externally motivated), they only remembered the material for one week and were less interested in it than were students who learned the material with no mention of a test (autonomously motivated). In states with high-stakes testing, the challenge for resilient classrooms is to help students identify multiple, alternative incentives for their learning without undue emphasis on a test. What happens when self-determination needs are not met in a classroom? When students' needs for autonomy are unfulfilled, they become angry, anxious, or bored; begin to fake doing schoolwork; and ultimately their performance declines (Miserandino, 1996).

What Are Classroom Routines and Practices That Strengthen Academic Self-Determination?

Self-determination is fostered in classrooms that emphasize the process of learning rather than the products of learning. Classroom practices that support student autonomy are those that allow students to choose the work that interests them, when and how they will learn it, the pace of their learning, and the standards that will be used to evaluate their work (Ames, 1992a; R. M. Ryan, Connell, & Deci, 1985). This is not to imply that students should be left to work completely on their own, but rather that they should be supported in gradually assuming more and more responsibility for decisions related to their learning. Students will frequently need assistance in formulating the goals that are meaningful to them and give direction to their efforts (Ames, 1992b; Assor, Kaplan, & Roth, 2002). In some cases, this assistance may be provided within the classroom context, such as posters on the wall that guide students through task completion, bulletin board reminders of due dates, or posted schedules that describe when and how to ask for help. Because these practices can be embedded into the daily routines of the classroom, they can exert a consistent and subtle influence that grooms the students to become self-directed, responsible learners.

Meaningfulness is an integral part of task design and instructional delivery in resilient classrooms. When students perceive that an activity is personally meaningful and addresses their own learning goals, they naturally focus more strongly on understanding the content and improving their skills. Their focus will be stronger yet when the content is so related to everyday life that students can say to themselves, "This is for me" (Brophy, 1999, p. 78).

Active student learning is also promoted by instruction that requires students to understand new information at a deep level by asking for justification of their responses to questions and by requiring effortful activity during the instruction (Middleton & Midgley, 2002). Deep processing makes students aware of instances when they are not really understanding the information, and the requirements for active participation make it more difficult for students to engage in unproductive behaviors while learning.

"Cognitive apprenticeships" can embed instruction in self-determination into subject curriculum by first modeling learning strategies for students and then helping them master the skill through coaching and scaffolding (Randi & Corno, 2000). For example, five specific strategies were incorporated into a secondary humanities course: (1) giving flexible assignments that allowed student choice; (2) building student learning communities through explicit instruction in cooperative learning skills; (3) providing explicit, scaffolded instruction in learning strategies; (4) using self- and peer evaluations and qualitative feedback to plan ways to improve performance; and (5) continuously assessing learning with curriculum-embedded probes similar to curriculum-based assessment (Deno, 1985, 2002; Deno, Fuchs, Marston, & Shin, 2001). At the same time, other self-regulation strategies were taught implicitly through the curriculum. Students were led to identify self-regulation strategies that characters used in the stories that they read. When students wrote essays connecting story characters to their own goal-oriented efforts, almost all of the students wrote papers with several examples of how they had used self-management strategies in their own studies. The teacher's ultimate goal was that students would develop more strategies of their own once they became accustomed to directing their own learning.

A Classroom Illustration

The seventh-grade math team at an urban middle school was concerned about low homework and test grades in one of the classes. While the students believed they had the skills to do the work, they were actually having limited success on weekly exams. The teachers were concerned that the students' false sense of confidence had convinced them that they could skip the homework and still make a good grade on the test. After they were shown the class data, the students reluctantly agreed that if they wanted to make better grades in math they were going to have to do the homework, but they also wanted to make doing the homework more fun. The students put themselves into three teams, made a chart with a team name, and created spaces to keep track of how many homework problems each team member attempted per day. Rather than competing based on the number of problems completed or accurately answered, which might have penalized some teams, they decided to compete based on "improvement scores": the difference between the number of problems attempted on two consecutive days. Also, a class goal was set to attempt at least one more problem each day than was attempted the day before. The students reported that the competition made doing the homework fun, and their weekly test grades improved.

BEHAVIORAL SELF-CONTROL

Disruptive, unproductive student behavior in classrooms reduces academic learning time for all students and limits the time available for instruction. In resilient classrooms, students are taught to manage their own behavior with the help of classroom routines that cue appropriate behavior. Self-management strategies and their supporting routines can be embedded into the daily life of the classroom so that they become self-sustaining.

How Does Effective Behavioral Self-Control Support Student Success?

Behavioral self-control is often discussed as if it were a set of skills that could be taught directly to children in the same way as spelling words, throwing a baseball, or weaving a tapestry are taught. In fact, behavioral self-control also depends very much on students' internalized preferences for behaving in specific ways, the results they hope to achieve through their behavior, and the subjective criteria that they use to assess whether their behavior meets their own standards (Bandura, 1989; Bear, Telzrow, & deOliveira, 1997). These values, preferences, and standards cannot be acquired through a discrete, 8-week course in social skills. Instead, they emerge out of the experiences that children bring with them from their homes, communities, and previous years in school.

When a classroom's students cooperate with classroom norms, their interactions with the teacher will be more satisfying. Teachers prefer students who are cooperative, conforming, cautious, and responsible. Attentive, regulated, and persistent students receive higher grades from their teacher (McDermott, Mordell, & Stoltzfus, 2001). Students who are argumentative, disruptive, or make inappropriate demands for attention are often treated negatively and receive less one-to-one instruction (Wentzel, 1991b). Notably, disciplined behavior predicts grades better than measures of verbal and nonverbal ability, suggesting that good conduct can often compensate for limited ability (McDermott et al., 2001). This has also been found in other studies, where grade retention, placement in special education classes, and dropping out are strongly predicted by behavior independent of intellectual ability (Safer, 1986).

Still, disruptive behaviors can sometimes be an artifact of insensitive classroom routines and practices, and a classroom's students and teacher can frequently identify cooperative solutions that eliminate the need for disruptive behaviors. For example, a fifth-grade class was housed in a temporary classroom and the teacher complained that the students were frequently out of their seats and whispering to one another during the daily mathematics lesson. A classroom discussion revealed that there was an irritating glare on the blackboard making it very difficult to see the board from the students' desks. The disruption was diminished substantially by changing the color of the chalk and installing a window shade. Strategies that include students in a classroom's governance will enhance students' autonomy and encourage their behavioral self-control.

In effect, behavioral self-control serves as the conduit between social and academic self-efficacy and goal setting. Without the ability to direct their behavior consistent with their own standards, students who set ambitious goals may not be able to act in ways that make them successful. Moreover, without the successes, students' academic and social efficacy can falter. Even though we have discussed these characteristics separately, their impact is inextricably linked.

What Are Classroom Routines and Practices That Strengthen Behavioral Self-Control?

Behavioral self-control begins with expectations for behavior that are developed cooperatively with students early in the school year. These conversations focus on the rules and routines that will allow students to act in self-determined ways and experience efficacy-building successes. After the expectations and rules become integrated into the routine of the classroom, students will generally adopt them as their own and act on them independently. Proactive classroom management provides specific techniques for teaching behavioral expectations, routines, and rules to students (Sugai, Horner, & Gresham, 2002). These include directly teaching students the expectation or rule using carefully sequenced positive and negative examples and role play, arranging opportunities for students to practice the routine, and monitoring student performance and providing reinforcement or corrective feedback.

Instructional practices that promote active student engagement in learning also support behavioral self-control. Some of these practices include making sure that activities are interesting and paced so that there is very little wasted time, keeping students busy with responding frequently, and using independent and one-on-one instructional groupings (Greenwood, Maheady, & Delquadri, 2002).

Peers can also support classmates to behave appropriately. One program, called Classwide Peer-Assisted Self-Management (CWPASM; Mitchem, Young, West, & Benyo, 2001), taught middle school students self-management skills, social skills, self-monitoring, and a reinforcement procedure, then assigned the students to two-person teams. Students rated themselves and their partners at regular intervals on how well they performed self-control behaviors. CWPASM led to improvements not only in the target behaviors but also in social competence for all students and for at-risk students who demonstrated high rates of disruptive behavior. The gains were maintained after the CWPASM structure was withdrawn.

Other programs use peers as effective mediators of both academic and behavioral tasks. Reciprocal Peer Tutoring (Fantuzzo & Rohrbeck, 1992) uses student-set academic goals, interdependent group reward contingencies, and reciprocal peer tutoring to improve elementary students' academic achievement and classroom behavior. Classwide Peer Tutoring (Greenwood, Delquadri, & Hall, 1989; Greenwood et al., 2002) uses structured tutor–tutee pairs to increase self-control behaviors such as "raising hands" and "academic talk."

A Classroom Illustration

Students in a second-grade classroom agreed that everyone had some behavior that could be improved to make the class run smoother, such as paying attention or not interrupting. Each student was able to identify one behavior that he or she thought could be improved. The teacher paired each student with a partner, called a "behavior buddy," based on the pair's complementary strengths, and taught everyone how to give feedback on behavior in ways that were positive and supportive. The teacher also asked how he could improve the classroom. The students told him that it was hard to pay attention when the pencil sharpener was always being used and that the way they lined up to go out for recess created a lot of shoving to be the first in line to get outside and grab a ball. The pencil sharpener distraction was eliminated by placing cans of sharpened pencils at various places in the room so that students could walk a shorter distance to exchange their dull pencil for a sharp one. The class also created a sign-up sheet so that students would take turns playing with all the playground equipment, including the balls. The students stayed in their behavior buddy groups for three weeks. A follow-up assessment showed that more students were paying attention and fewer were interrupting, matching the teacher's observation that the classroom was running smoother.

SUMMARY

In this chapter, we provided an elaborated explanation of the ways in which students' self-agency emerges out of classroom routines and practices, and the impact that enhanced self-agency has on student learning. For purposes of clarity, this explanation separated out students' feelings about their performance (academic efficacy), the plans and intentions that guide their performance (self-determination), and their ability to act upon these plans (behavioral self-control). In reality, though, these different aspects of self-agency are mutually interdependent, and classroom practices that strengthen any one of the self-agency characteristics frequently strengthen the others as well. We recognize that this focus on students' autonomy and self-sufficiency can seem out of place in authoritarian classrooms that emphasize teachers as the ultimate authorities and decision makers. Ultimately, if students are to emerge from public education as self-sufficient and autonomous adults, the seeds of their autonomy must be planted in the earliest elementary grades and nourished carefully throughout the 13 years of their public education.

ONE MORE EXAMPLE: CHANGING CLASSROOM AGENCY

Mrs. M's second-grade classroom had a reputation for chaos. During one morning math period, two students were out of their seats sharpening pencils, two more were tugging on Mrs. M's sleeve and complaining that each had stolen the other's pencil, a fifth student was tussling with his neighbor over a dictionary, and three more were wandering aimlessly about the room. A few very distractible students were especially disrupted by the classroom's din and had been placed on individual behavior programs to increase their attention to learning tasks. Anonymous student surveys confirmed the school psychologists' observations: although students thought that they followed the class rules most of the time, they didn't think that their classmates did. Just as important, they didn't think they understood how to do their work in the class, couldn't tell when they'd made mistakes, and weren't sure how to fix their mistakes once they noticed them. The classroom's chaos was not only disrupting students' work but was making it difficult for them to develop skills for self-managing their own learning.

It was clear that a first step was helping the class figure out routines that everyone could follow to maintain order in the class. Following the procedures of Witt, La Fleur, Naquin, and Gilbertson (1999), one routine was taught each week. First, steps for the routine were posted on the blackboard and discussed with the class during a morning meeting. In a few cases, the class suggested minor revisions to the routines that would make them more effective. Then, the routine was practiced during the morning's seatwork time while the school psychologist gave the class simple prompts and reminders, and feedback on their performance. For the rest of the week, the class practiced the routine without the school psychologists' help. In this way, routines were established for stopping and paying attention to the teacher, trading dull for sharpened pencils during seatwork time, following teacher directions, asking for and getting help, and picking up and turning in papers.

The most immediate impact was on students' conduct: disciplinary "think times" dropped from an average of five or six per day to an average of two or three per day. Just as important, students began to show more confidence in their work. On anonymous surveys, they reported that they could do as well as most kids in the class and were more comfortable with hard work. Still, they continued to report that they couldn't tell when they'd made mistakes and weren't sure how to fix them.

Mrs. M shifted the topic of the weekly class meetings, discussing the strategies that students could use to evaluate and improve their own work. At the class's suggestion, she began to post "keys" for most assignments next to a cup full of red pens. Once students completed their seatwork, they could take their own assignment over to the correcting table, check it against the key, and mark their own errors. Once they'd done that, they were welcome to take the paper back to their desk and correct their mistakes. The class also created a new rule for working: try it yourself, ask a friend for help, and ask at least one other classmate before asking the teacher. Because they were using each other as tutors, students became adept at describing "tricks" or strategies that they used and at borrowing each others' tricks.

ANNOTATED BIBLIOGRAPHY

Bandura, A. (1993). Perceived self-efficacy in cognitive development and functioning. *Educational Psychologist, 28*(2), 117–148.

This elegantly written article by Albert Bandura describes the effects of self-efficacy beliefs on cognitive processes, motivation, and affective processes such as depression and anxiety, and how efficacy beliefs influence choice of activities and environments that determine life courses. He outlines the impact of efficacy beliefs on students' social and emotional developmental trajectories and the role of teachers' efficacy in student academic achievement. His discussion of collective school efficacy shows that faculties who believe in their collective ability to educate and motivate their students can produce high achievement in their students, even in schools that contain students from predominantly minority and low socioeconomic status backgrounds.

Deci, E. L., Vallerand, R. J., Pelletier, L. G., & Ryan, R. M. (1991). Motivation and education: The self-determination perspective. *Educational Psychologist, 26,* 325–346.

This article is good background reading for those who are unfamiliar with Deci's theory of intrinsic and extrinsic motivation and how it develops. The authors also present a detailed discussion of how the social context of the school supports self-determination of both students and teachers. Specific suggestions for intervening to promote self-determination are included.

Fantuzzo, J. W., & Rohrbeck, C. A. (1992). Self-managed groups: Fitting self-management approaches into classroom systems. *School Psychology Review, 21,* 255–263.

This article presents an intervention strategy applied to an urban elementary classroom that combines self-management methods, group interdependent reward contingencies, and reciprocal peer teaching to promote academic and social competency. Students experienced gains in math achievement, perceived academic competency, and self-control. The intervention is presented in enough detail to permit implementation after reading the article.

Mitchem, K. J., Young, K. R., West, R. P., & Benyo, J. (2001). CWPASM: A Classwide Peer-Assisted Self-Management Program for general education classrooms. *Education and Treatment of Children, 24*, 111–141.

The authors show how on-task behavior and social skills use was improved in three language arts classrooms of general education seventh graders and 10 target at-risk students. The teacher taught students self-management skills, social skills, and a set of CWPASM procedures that are clearly presented in the article. Both students and the teacher rated the intervention as highly acceptable and feasible. There is a clear description of the multiple baseline design with systematic withdrawal to test maintenance, making the article valuable from a methodological standpoint.

Pintrich, P. R. (2000). Multiple goals, multiple pathways: The role of goal orientation in learning and achievement. *Journal of Educational Psychology, 92*(3), 544–555.

Pintrich discusses the normative model of goal orientation wherein mastery goals promote and performance goals work against motivation and achievement. He then presents research on revised goal theory. In this revised model, students can have multiple goals, including simultaneous goals of mastery and performance, which result in adaptive outcomes. Classroom implications for development of self-efficacy, positive and negative affect related to school, adaptive risk taking, and cognitive strategy use are presented for students who exhibit various combinations of mastery and performance goals.

Roeser, R. W., Midgley, C., & Urdan, T. C. (1996). Perceptions of the school psychological environment and early adolescents' psychological and behavioral functioning in school: The mediating role of goals and belonging. *Journal of Educational Psychology, 88*, 408–422.

Although the focus of this article is on the achievement goal characteristics (task mastery vs. performance goals) and quality of teacher–student relationships in middle schools, the information is relevant to elementary classrooms as well. The article describes these complex relationships thoroughly and concludes that the incentive programs in schools, such as honor rolls and special privileges for brighter students, undermine students' feelings of belonging and belief in their chance to be successful. Examples of the questions used to explore schoolwide perceptions parallel the anonymous surveys we have used with students.

Schraw, G., Flowerday, T., & Lehman, S. (2001). Increasing situational interest in the classroom. *Educational Psychology Review, 13*, 211–223.

Behavioral self-control of students is not only a function of strategies employed by students but also reflects qualities of the instructional environment that are under the teacher's control. The authors present ways to increase the situational, or spontaneous, interest value of the classroom such as offering meaningful choices to students, selecting vivid, well-organized texts containing content that fits with students' prior experience, encouraging use of specific and general study strategies that promote active learning, and providing relevance cues to capture the attention of low-interest students. When students are actively engaged in learning, there is less opportunity or motivation to engage in off-task or disruptive behavior.

Zimmerman, B. J. (2000). Self-efficacy: An essential motive to learn. *Contemporary Educational Psychology, 25*, 82–91.

This article by a prominent researcher of self-efficacy defines the concept of self-efficacy, distinguishes it from related conceptions such as outcome expectations and locus of control, and describes its role in academic motivation and learning. He discusses how teachers can improve the efficacy beliefs of their students through, for example, adult modeling of cognitive strategy use and asking students to set proximal goals.

5

Assessing the Resilience of Classrooms

Assessment is essential to the formation of resilient classrooms. Through assessment, the characteristics of classroom resilience are measured, counted, and quantified so that they become visible to the classroom's teachers and students. Once they are visible, the characteristics can then be strengthened, extended, and infused into daily classroom routines and practices. Without assessment, the characteristics of resilience can only be discussed as abstract principles that are important for student learning but have little practical impact on daily classroom activities. Thus, a critical first step in enhancing classroom resilience is to assess existing classroom characteristics in order to define the goals of intervention and create a baseline against which progress can be measured.

Strategies for assessing classroom resilience must be practical so that teachers will readily adopt them as useful teaching tools. That is, measures of the six classroom characteristics must be brief so that administration of the assessment does not disrupt essential learning activities in the classroom. They must be simple to code and analyze so that the assessment is time efficient. They must be easily graphed, because graphs of classroom assessment data make it possible for teachers and students to understand and plan from the information. Finally, the measures must have good face validity so that the relevance of their results is self-evident to the teachers and students.

Classroom assessment strategies must also have strong psychometric properties so that their results are convincing to external audiences for classroom data such as administrators, school boards, or community leaders. As evidence that they are reliable indices of the classroom characteristics, they need to demonstrate strong internal consistency and good test–retest reliability over brief intervals of time. Moreover, when the elements of resilience are altered within a classroom, the measures must be sensitive to these changes so that they can detect intervention effects. In order to capture successive changes in a classroom over time, the measures must be capable of repeated administrations without practice effects distorting the results. Further, to link the resilient classroom model to existing research, the brief measures of effective classrooms must be correlated with the more complex and comprehensive measures of classroom characteristics that were used in the original basic research.

In the past, efforts at classroom reform have suffered from a myopic emphasis on the perspectives of the teachers in the classroom, or of outside observers who were not classroom participants. The perspectives of the students who learn in the classrooms and of the students' families were sadly overlooked. An essential contribution of the resilient classroom assessment must be to assess characteristics from an ecological framework by capturing the perspectives of these overlooked classroom participants.

Finally, the assessment of classroom resilience must, by definition, assess the classroom contexts for learning rather than the needs and competencies of individual students in the classroom. This presents a special challenge since the majority of educational assessment tools are focused on individual students or teachers. Indeed, it requires a good deal of ingenuity to adapt existing measurement strategies to the assessment of classroom characteristics while still using strategies that are practical and empirically defensible.

In the remainder of this chapter, we describe several different strategies for assessing classroom resilience. First, we describe the important types of assessment that can assess classroom characteristics. Next, we summarize the major research measures that were used in basic developmental research on the resilience characteristics. Finally, we describe the ClassMaps surveys that we have developed and that we use to track the resilience characteristics in elementary and middle school classrooms. Copies of the ClassMaps surveys are provided in Appendix A, and information for ordering the other research measures is provided at the end of this chapter.

ASSESSMENT STRATEGIES

Classroom characteristics can be assessed through surveys and rating scales, systematic direct observations, or records and permanent products of classroom activities. Each of these assessment strategies carries its own unique advantages and inaccuracies. Surveys and rating scales are criticized for being indirect measures, capturing the impressions and imprecise memories of the person who completes the scales. However, in some cases, rating scales provide a more powerful index of a classroom's characteristics because they reflect the accumulated experience of people who are highly familiar with the classroom and are less reactive to single isolated events that might occur. Ratings will be most accurate and useful when the person completing the rating knows the information requested by the rating scale, when questions are carefully worded to be understandable and precise, and when the rating form is sufficiently brief so that raters do not find it tedious to complete. Ratings can be adapted to assess classroom characteristics by carefully planning the questions and by aggregating the results across multiple raters. They can be ecologically broad measures when they are collected from all participants in a classroom.

Systematic observations are highly valued because they provide objective information about events or activities in a classroom. However, the collection of reliable observation data requires substantial discipline on the part of the observer, who must be strict in following a preplanned observational protocol. Further, completion of a single, systematic observation may not be sufficient to provide reliable data about an event (Doll & Elliott, 1994). Instead, multiple observations may need to be collected on more than one day to secure a representative sample of classroom activities. More important, observations can only be used when the phenomena under study are visible to someone who is not a participant in the classroom. Observations will be most reliable when the observation protocol is simple, when observers have been trained to follow the protocol, and when observer reliability is assessed on an ongoing basis while data is collected. To assess classroom characteristics, observations should be collected across multiple participants in the classroom.

In some cases, the permanent records of a classroom can be used as classroom assessment data. For example, information about attendance and tardy rates, work completion, and work performance is frequently available in a teacher's class record book. Information about work quality or work completion might be gathered by examining papers that were turned in by the classroom's students. The number, frequency, and nature of office discipline reports can sometimes provide an index of the behavioral conduct of a classroom. The most glaring weakness with permanent product assessment is that the collection of this information is not always as reliable as one might think. For example, in one middle school where we worked, school attendance records were highly inaccurate and incomplete. Alternatively, when class records are faithfully kept, they can present very useful assessment data that are very simple to collect.

RESEARCH MEASURES OF THE SIX CHARACTERISTICS

Teacher–Student Relationships

Much of the research on teacher's relationships with their students used Pianta's (2001a) Student–Teacher Relationship Scale. This is a 28-item teacher-report scale that provides information about three dimensions of relationships: the degree to which the teacher and student are in conflict, the teacher's feelings of closeness and affection toward the student, and the student's overdependence on the teacher. The scale has been normed on 1,500 students and 275 teachers in grades preschool through third grade. The internal consistency of its Conflict (alpha = .92) and Closeness (alpha = .86) subscales is strong, but the Dependency subscale is less so (alpha = .64). Similarly, test–retest reliabilities were stronger for the Conflict (r = .92) and Closeness (r = .88) subscales than for the Dependency subscale (r = .76). Validity studies have shown that the scale predicts academic success or failure (Hamre & Pianta, 2001; Pianta, 1999). The most obvious shortcoming of this scale for assessing classroom resilience is its reliance on teacher reports. It would be unreasonably tedious for a teacher to complete the 28 items for all students in a class, and the reliance on teacher perspectives omits information about the student experiences of those relationships.

An observational assessment of a classroom's peer relationships and teacher–student relationships is incorporated into the Classroom Systems Observation Scale (Fish & Dane, 2000). This is a 47-item scale that applies family systems theories to the observation of relationships within a classroom. An outside observer spends 45 minutes in the classroom making notes about three features: cohesion or the emotional bonding and supportiveness among students and teachers, flexibility and student participation in the teacher's discipline and decision making, and the clarity and openness of communication among students and between students and the teacher. Preliminary investigations have shown good interobserver agreement for the Cohesion (kappa = .83) and Flexibility (kappa = .89) subscales, with less agreement for the Communication subscale (kappa = .61). Similarly, test–retest reliability was strongest for the Cohesion (r = .77) and Flexibility (r = .79) subscales. An obvious advantage of this scale is its identification of observable classroom actions that relate to stronger interpersonal relationships. Still, its shortcoming is its lack of validity information. Work is still ongoing to link to the scale to student outcomes and classroom learning.

Peer Relationships

Sociometric measures of a classroom's peer relationships are among the oldest measures of a classroom's ecological system. Sociometric measures of children's competence with peers were developed in the 1930s and used widely in schools throughout the 1950s to describe the social climate of classrooms (Barclay, 1992; Gresham, 1986). Subsequently these formed the basis for substantial research on children's peer relationships in the 1980s and 1990s. Their validity, reliability, and stability as measures of peer acceptance and social competence is well established (Bukowski, Hoza, & Newcomb, 1994; Gresham, 1986; Hoza, Molina, Bukowski, & Sippola, 1995; Parker & Asher, 1993).

Sociometric assessments can use either peer nomination strategies, in which students list their classmates who match a description (e.g., "friends," "like to play with"), or roster-rating strategies in which students rate each classmate according to a criterion (e.g., "like to play with"; Asher & Hymel, 1986; Berndt, 1984; Parker & Asher, 1993). Peer nomination strategies sometimes limit the number of classmates that a student can name (e.g., "your three best friends") and sometimes ask for negative instead of positive nominations (e.g., "the children you do *not* like to play with"). Roster ratings are generally preferred because they reflect a student's overall acceptance by every other student in the class (Parker & Asher, 1993) and appear to be more reliable than nominations (Asher & Hymel, 1986; Parker & Asher, 1989, 1993). When nominations are used, limited-choice nominations that restrict the number of classmates a student is allowed to name are problematic because they underidentify mutual friendships and can artificially lower the measure of peer acceptance (Parker & Asher, 1993). Still, both sociometric ratings and nominations have been shown to be stable over time and across situations (Coie & Kupersmidt, 1983; Berndt, 1984; Newcomb & Bukowski, 1984; Parker & Asher, 1989, 1993).

When either roster-rating or peer nomination procedures are used, the peer acceptance of any single student in a class can be determined by counting the number of nominations that he or she receives or computing his or her average peer ratings (Coie, Dodge, & Coppotelli, 1982; Parker & Asher, 1993). Peer friendships can be identified if two students nominate or give high ratings to each other (Berndt, 1981; Berndt & Perry, 1986). Sociometric measures are especially suitable for describing the peer social climate of a classroom, either by computing the average sociometric rating that classmates give to one another or by computing the average number of positive and negative nominations given and received using unlimited list procedures. (An extensive history of school applications of sociometry can be found in Barclay, 1992.)

Home–School Relationships

The National Parent–Teacher Association (1997) has created a 55-item checklist that describes quality indicators of effective home–school relationships. The checklist includes items describing home–school communication, promotion of parenting, parents' role in student learning, volunteering opportunities, parent participation in school decision making, and collaboration with the broader community. The checklist is intended as an informal rather than formal assessment, and no information is available about its reliability or its prediction of student success. Alternatively, the Illinois State Board of Education (1994) developed a 30-item Parent Involvement Inventory to assess school practices that foster home–school relationships. The inventory is intended for use by parents or educators and asks questions about specific school practices that help parents support student learning, encourage volunteering, communicate with families, provide for adult learning of parents and teachers, promote family advocacy and decision making, and foster home–school partnerships. Again, no information is available about the inventory's reliability or validity. In both cases, these are intended to assess schoolwide support for home–school relationships and would need to be modified to assess classroom-level support.

Self-Determination

The AIR Self-Determination Scale (American Institutes for Research, 1994) is a research tool developed to assess the self-determination of students with disabilities, identify their strengths and areas needing improvement, and guide strategies for enhancing their autonomy. The scale's subscales follow a general problem-solving model, assessing how prepared students are to articulate their needs, set goals, make choices, act on those choices, and review the results of their actions before revising their plans. Alternative rating forms are available for use by teachers (30 items), students (24 items), and parents (18 items). In each case, raters use a 5-point Likert scale to describe how frequently the student demonstrates each behavior (where 1 = never and 5 = always). A preliminary version of the scale was field-tested in California and New York with 70 schools and more than 450 students with and without disabilities. Results showed that the scales had good internal consistency (alternate items correlations ranging from .91 to .98) and strong test–retest reliabilities over a 3-month interval ($r = .74$). Still, no information was provided about the degree to which adult ratings of students' self-determination matched the students' self-ratings. Factor analysis confirmed the scale's subscale structure, but evidence of the scale's external validity is still being gathered. The AIR scale's use of multiple raters allows for a broad assessment of self-determination, but its focus on individual student planning restricts its utility for classwide assessment. This question is of special importance for classroom assessment since, while it would be impractical to ask teachers to complete the 30-item scale for each of their students, the student-report scale could be gathered from a full class and results could be aggregated across all students in that class.

Academic Efficacy

Research describing the academic efficacy of students in school has used numerous different measures. Pintrich and DeGroot (1990) borrowed from several of these to construct a 56-item rating scale called the Motivated Strategies for Learning Questionnaire (MSLQ). Students complete the MSLQ using a 7-point Likert scale (where 1 = not true at all for me and 7 = very true of me). The 9-item Self-Efficacy subscale was included in the MSLQ, and additional subscales were included for Intrinsic Value, Test Anxiety, Strategy Use, and Self-Regulation. The internal consistency reliability of the subscales was respectable, ranging from .74 to a high of .89 for the Self-Efficacy subscale. The subscale scores correlated modestly but significantly with student report cards, seatwork, exams, and essays. The MSLQ is a reasonable individual measure of academic efficacy.

Behavioral Self-Control

The Student Observation System of the Behavior Assessment System for Children (BASC/SOS; Reynolds & Kamphaus, 1992) uses a momentary time sampling system to collect observations of children's classroom behaviors. The observational protocol provides a comprehensive, well-organized list of adaptive and maladaptive classroom behaviors. The behaviors were categorized, sorted according to frequency, and then organized into four appropriate and nine inappropriate behavior categories. A 15-

minute observation period consists of thirty 30-second intervals. During each interval, observers spend the first 3 seconds observing the child and the remaining 27 seconds checking each behavior that occurred on the observation sheet. Then, at the end of the 15-minute period, the observer completes a brief rating form describing all behaviors that occurred. One strength of the BASC/SOS is its well-conceptualized list of classroom behaviors. It is an efficient strategy for recording the behavior of a single child but would have to be adapted to record the multiple behaviors of all children in a class.

Summary

While these research measures provide reliable and valid assessments of each of the characteristics of resilient classrooms, most do not assess these as properties of classrooms. Instead, the focus of prior research has been on the contribution of individual student and teacher characteristics to the learning that occurs in classrooms. Still, it is possible to adapt individual measures to the task of assessing classroom contexts. Surveys and rating forms can be collected from multiple students in a class and aggregated across all students to describe the whole class. Teacher reports are more difficult to convert to classwide measures. It is tedious for teachers to complete rating forms on every one of their students. However, Asher (1995) has collected teacher ratings for an entire class by writing a question across the top of a page (e.g., "Who often picks on and teases other students?") and listing the students in the class below. Teachers complete the rating by circling the names of students in answer to the question. Observation protocols that were designed to assess a single student can sometimes be adapted to classwide observation by systematically observing a different student in the class during each interval of the observation. Interpretations of these modified measures must be made with caution. Since such modifications would alter the psychometric properties of the measures, it would be important to reassess the reliability and validity of the measurement strategies in their altered format.

CLASSMAPS SURVEYS: AN ALTERNATIVE ASSESSMENT STRATEGY

The limited availability of practical and empirically supported measures of classroom resilience has prompted us to develop an alternative assessment strategy that we call "ClassMaps" (Doll, Zucker, & Brehm, 1999a; Zucker, Brehm, & Doll, 2000). ClassMaps are brief, anonymous student surveys modeled after the sociometric rating procedures in which children rate their classmates according to specific characteristics (Asher & Hymel, 1986; Parker & Asher, 1993). Students' sociometric ratings have been shown to provide highly accurate descriptions of their classmates' social strengths, social weaknesses, and interpersonal roles (Asher & Hymel, 1986; Coie & Kupersmidt, 1983; Parker & Asher, 1989). This suggested that students might also be able to provide accurate descriptions of their classroom's resilience. To adapt the sociometric strategy to assessing classrooms, we wrote brief surveys that asked all students in a class to rate their classroom in terms of the six resilience characteristics: academic efficacy, academic self-determination, behavioral self-control, teacher–student relationships, peer relationships, and home–school relationships. Individual student ratings could then be aggregated across all students to provide a classroom measure. Copies of the ClassMaps surveys are included in Appendix A.

The ClassMaps surveys were developed through a systematic piloting procedure (Doll et al., 1999a; Doll, Zucker, & Brehm, 1999b; Zucker et al., 2000). Drafts of the items were composed from the research for each of the six characteristics of resilient classrooms. Then, the surveys were administered to a large group of middle school students and were modified to ensure that they were easy to understand and contributed important information. The item format was adjusted so that students understood how to respond quickly and easily. The administration time was monitored closely, and the survey length was adjusted so that most classes could complete all six surveys in 20 minutes or less. The internal consistency of the surveys was examined, as well as their factor structure and their relations to external indices of student success: grades, attendance, and work completion rates. Then, the surveys were refined in response to these analyses and the process was repeated with a large group of elementary school students. Statistical analyses again identified weak items that required revision, while advice from elementary school students and teachers guided further refinements in the survey language and formats. A summary of the reliability and validity information from these studies is summarized in Table 5.1.

All ClassMaps surveys follow a common format. Each question is followed by three choices: yes, sometimes, and no. Students are asked to circle the choice that is true for them. For example:

I like school.

Yes Sometimes No

Responses are coded by assigning 2 points for every "Yes," 1 point for every "Sometimes," and 0 points for every "No" for each of the six items. Total scores could range from 0 ("No" circled for every item) to 12–18 ("Yes" circled for all items). The Believing in Me survey assesses academic efficacy in a class by asking students about how they feel about their schoolwork and their expectations of success. The Taking Charge survey assesses academic self-determination by asking students about their participation in goal setting and decision making related to their learning. The Following the Class Rules survey assesses behavioral self-control by asking students about their own behavior and that of their classmates. The My Teacher survey assesses teacher–student relationship by asking students about their experiences interacting with their teacher in class. The My Classmates survey assesses peer relationships by asking students about their interactions with their fellow students in class, at lunch, and at recess. The

TABLE 5.1. Reliability and Validity Data for the ClassMaps Surveys

	Middle school data[a]					Elementary school data[b]		
			Correlations with					
Characteristics	Items	Alpha	Absences	Work completion	Grade point	Items	Individual alpha	Class alpha
Academic efficacy	6	.89	–.142**	.173**	.240**	6	.64	.79
Self-determination	6	.93	–.064	.108*	.149**	7	.55	.75
Behavioral self-control	[There was no self-control survey at the time of this study.]					8	.75	.93
Teacher–student relationships	7	.82	–.114*	–.004	.084	6	.84	.92
Peer relationships	7	.56	–.009	.112*	.105*	7	.70	.71
Home–school relationships	8	.77	–.255**	.186**	.275**	6	.77	.82

[a]Doll, Zucker, and Brehm (1999a).
[b]Doll, Siemers, and Brey (2003).
*$p < .05$; **$p < .01$.

Talking with My Parents survey assesses home–school communication by asking students how much they talk with their parents about school.

We have used the ClassMaps surveys with classrooms from the second through the eighth grades. Students have repeatedly said that it is very important to let them know why the surveys are being collected and how their information will be used. Consequently, the following instructions are used when collecting the ClassMaps surveys:

> These papers will ask you about your classroom. When we're done, we'll gather all your answers together and make them into a graph. Here is an example from another class like yours. (*Show a transparency of a data graph that was collected from another class and point to it during the explanation.*) This is what a group of fourth graders said about their class. The graph shows that lots of kids were not having fun at recess and too many kids had arguments or no one to play with. Using this information, the class decided to plan some new and different games at recess, and found ways to include everyone in the class in the games. This is what the fourth graders said after they had used their plan for several months. (*Uncover the "after" graph on the transparency.*)
>
> Once we have graphs for your class, your teacher and I will bring them to class to show you. Then, you and your teacher can plan ways to make your class better, using the information from the surveys.
>
> Please DO NOT put your name on your papers. We don't need to know who wrote each paper, and no one will know which paper is yours. Instead, your teacher

needs to know what the whole class thinks. There are no right or wrong answers. (Doll, Siemers, Song, & Nickolite, 2002, p. 10)

The simplest way to analyze a classroom's surveys is to compute frequencies (the number of times each response is given) or percentages (the percentage of times each response is given) for each survey question. Results can then be graphed using a common computer graphing program. Simple bar graphs can describe results for each of the six surveys, using a single stacked bar for each question. The bottom stack shows "Yes" responses, and the top stack shows "Sometimes" responses. It is not necessary to also show the "No" responses since these are a mathematical derivative of the "Yes," "Sometimes," and "Total" responses. An example of a ClassMaps graph for the My Classmates (peer relationships) survey is included in Figure 5.1. Labeling each bar in the graph with the abbreviated question makes it very easy to interpret the information. The ultimate purpose of these graphs is to accurately and quickly display results of the surveys for teachers and students.

AN ASSESSMENT EXAMPLE

The following example of a ClassMaps survey assessment was completed in a fourth-grade classroom. After looking at all of her survey results for all six surveys, the teacher decided to focus on the peer relationships in the classroom. She believed that there were one or two bullies in her class that were causing difficulties for most of the other students. (Figure 5.1 shows the ClassMaps graph at which she was looking.)

The students in the class interpreted this information differently than the teacher did. They thought that their difficulties stemmed from being a year-round school where their teacher "looped" with them. As a result, they had played together for several years. They thought that the teacher's "bullies" were new students who were struggling because the class did not do a good job of accepting them into their group. The class overlooked new classmates, did not remember to include them in games, and didn't show them how to enter into the "kid society" at their school. The students' solution was to create a Welcome Wagon program to cordially introduce new students to their class. They assigned one buddy a week to each new classmate for his or her first 4 weeks. The buddies' job was to include the new classmate in play, to introduce him or her to the school, and to make him or her feel welcome. Then the class wrote a manual for introducing new students to their school. They took their Welcome Wagon program around to other classrooms in the school, to explain what they were doing. Also, the chapter books that the class read in their literature and social studies lessons focused on friendship and making friends. Figure 5.2 shows what their ClassMaps survey looked like 6 months later. All students had friends at recess and lunch, and students were much more satisfied with their friendships and reported fewer fights and arguments in the class. In this example, the ClassMaps surveys allowed the teacher and the students to see the characteristics of their classroom and, once they were able

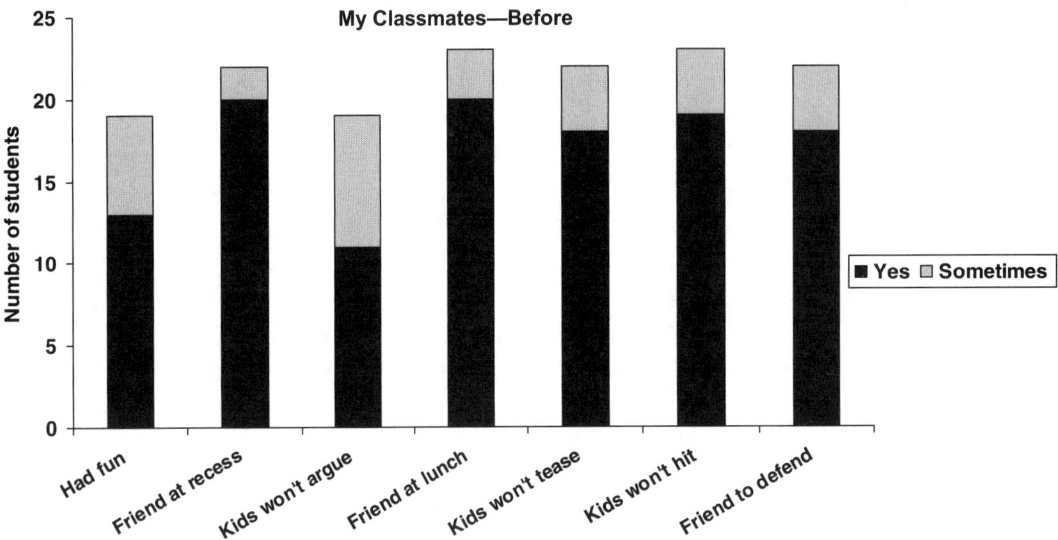

FIGURE 5.1. Example of a classroom's ClassMaps preintervention survey results for peer relationships.

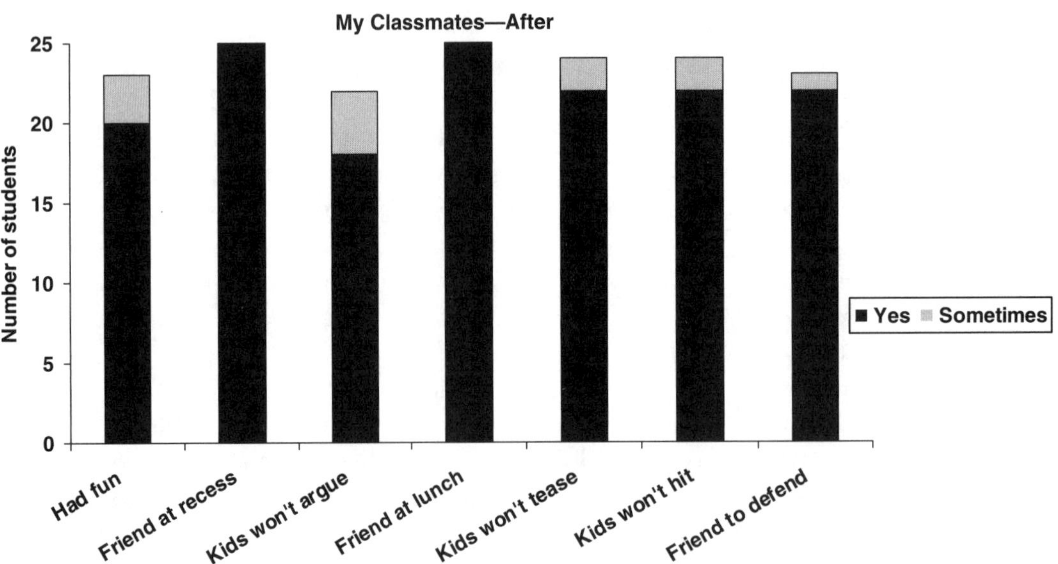

FIGURE 5.2. Example of a classroom's ClassMaps postintervention survey results for peer relationships.

to do that, they could plan for different routines and practices that would improve their class.

SUMMARY

This chapter has discussed alternative ways to assess classrooms, as a first step toward describing a classroom's strengths and weaknesses. The ultimate effect of these evaluations is to make social and self-regulatory characteristics visible to the teachers, classroom teams, and students who will be working to strengthen these. Chapter 6 explains how this information is used to guide subsequent interventions, and Chapter 7 explains how to make those results most accessible to students at different grades.

ORDERING INFORMATION

American Institutes for Research. (1994). *The AIR Self-Determination Scale.* New York: Columbia University. Order from the American Institutes for Research, 10720 Columbia Pike, Silver Spring, MD 20901.

Fish, M. C., & Dane, E. (2000). The Classroom Systems Observation Scale: Development of an instrument to assess classrooms using a systems perspective. *Learning Environments Research, 3,* 67–92. Order from Marian C. Fish, School of Education, Queens College of the City University of New York, Flushing, NY 11367.

Illinois State Board of Education. (1994). Parent Involvement Inventory. Available online through the website of the North Central Regional Education Laboratory, *http://www.ncrel.org/sdrs/areas/issues/envrnmnt/famncomm/pa4lk12.htm.*

National Parent–Teacher Association. (1997). National standards for parent/family involvement programs. Chicago: Author. Available online at *http://www.pta.org/programs/appenda.htm.*

Pianta, R. C. (2001). *Student–Teacher Relationship Scale.* Lutz, FL: Psychological Assessment Resources. Order from Psychological Assessment Resources, Inc., 16204 North Florida Avenue, Lutz, FL 33549, or online at *www.parinc.com.*

Reynolds, C. R., & Kamphaus, R. W. (1992). *The Behavior Assessment System for Children.* Circle Pines, MN: American Guidance Service. Order from American Guidance Service, 4201 Woodland Road, Circle Pines, MN 55014-1796, or online at *www.agsnet.com.*

6

Convening the Systems for Change

Transforming a typical classroom into a resilient classroom doesn't quite take a village, but it does require the combined efforts of many different people who participate in and contribute to the classroom ecology. Consequently, plans for change are most effective when they are made within a classroom team that is led by the teacher and that may include the school psychologist or counselor, a mentor teacher, a parent, and the classroom's students. This classroom team should be carefully selected so that it represents the classroom's ecology but is small enough to work efficiently and harmoniously. In this chapter, we recommend a collaborative consultation process that classroom teams can use to plan and implement classroom interventions. Collaboration is the preferable interaction style between coequal team members, and consultation is the process that enables team members to work together toward their shared goal for the classroom (Conoley & Conoley, 1992; Friend & Cook, 1997).

The procedures that underlie classroom consultation borrow from the extensive research on team consultation (Friend & Cook, 1997; Flugum & Reschly, 1994; Jayanthi & Friend, 1992; Meyers et al., 1996; Rosenfield, 1992; Telzrow et al., 2000). Team consultation uses a data-based problem-solving procedure in which problems are identified, analyzed through systematic data collection, and addressed with step-by-step interventions, and then the intervention is evaluated and modified as needed based upon data. The success of systematic team consultation has been directly related to the presence of eight quality indicators (Flugum & Reschly, 1994; Telzrow et al., 2000): precise problem definition, baseline data, clearly identified goals, hypothesized reasons for the problem, a systematic intervention plan, evidence of treatment integrity, data describing the response to treatment, and comparison of student performance with a baseline. Teams whose practices satisfy more of these quality indicators have greater impact on students' academic and behavioral success (Bahr, Whitten, Dieker, Kocarek, & Manson, 1999; Flugum & Reschly, 1994; Telzrow et al., 2000).

Classroom consultation differs from team consultation only in that its target is classroom characteristics rather than individual student behaviors. In this chapter, we presume that ClassMaps surveys will be used to support the consultation, but any of the other assessment procedures described in Chapter 5 can be substituted as long as they provide reliable and valid information about the classroom characteristics. Classroom consultation is built upon eight steps:

1. Assemble a classroom team that will work with the teacher to identify classroom goals, plan for change, and implement the plan.
2. Gather classroom data to identify strengths and weaknesses in the classroom's natural supports for learning.
3. Analyze the classroom data, and graph the data to highlight critical relationships.
4. Discuss the data with the classroom team, and use the data to identify a goal for improving the class.
5. Share selected portions of the data with the classroom's students, and listen to their hypotheses that explain the data and their ideas for intervention.
6. Convene the classroom team to create a written plan for classroom change, drawing upon the students' suggestions and the shared expertise of all team members.
7. Implement the plan while keeping careful records to show that the plan was followed.
8. Monitor progress of the classroom intervention by re-collecting classroom data at regular intervals and by refining the plan in response to classroom data.

The remainder of this chapter discusses these steps in more detail. Throughout the chapter, we assume that the commitment to building resilient classrooms will be initiated by a classroom consultant who is not the teacher, but this is not always the case. Several of our own case examples come from teachers who initiated the change process in their own classrooms, convened a team to help them, and directed the change process with the help of their team. In some cases, a full school of teachers will become engaged in promoting resilient classrooms within the building. While this chapter discusses the process from the perspective of a single classroom, Chapter 10 briefly discusses the process of introducing classroom consultation to a full school.

STEP 1: PLANNING FOR CHANGE

The first step begins when a consultant gives the teacher an overview of the classroom change process and an explanation of how enhancing resiliency can improve classroom relationships and achievement. To prepare for this, classroom consultants should read Chapters 1 through 5, reframing them into words that will be most relevant to the teacher. Reading selected references from the annotated bibliography can further expand the consultant's understanding. Thorough preparation gives consultants confidence and allows them to answer questions promptly and knowledgeably.

Teachers' participation in classroom consultation must be voluntary, and any classroom data that are collected must be kept confidential. In every case example in this book, we secured the principal's prior agreement that classroom data would belong to the teacher and would not be shown outside the classroom by anyone except the teacher. This ensured that the classroom consultation process would not be transformed into an exercise in teacher evaluation.

Once the teacher understands how the students will benefit from the process and what is involved, the consultant and the teacher assemble a small classroom team to assist with future planning and decision making. Team members could include another teacher who is a peer mentor, a paraeducator or other support personnel who work in the classroom, or a parent of one of the students in the class. Although their participation can complicate scheduling, parents have a unique understanding of how to coordinate home–school communication and can rally support of other parents when intervention begins. In some cases, the team members will meet briefly to review data collection procedures and learn about the teacher's purpose in asking for their help.

Finally, the teacher and the team will plan to collect data about the classroom's characteristics. It is important to show teachers how the classroom data relate to other kinds of data that they already have to describe their classroom and to consider the relative reliability and validity of all sources of classroom data. When classroom data are used for instructional purposes only, most school districts do not require a formal approval process. However, in every case, we sent a letter home to parents that told them about the project and how the survey information would be used. (Of course, if there are plans to publish classroom data as part of a larger research study, the consultant must follow formal research approval requirements for obtaining parental consent and ensuring confidentiality.)

During this first step and throughout classroom consultation, it is important to follow the teacher's lead, even if it deviates from the recommended process. Teachers are ultimately held responsible for the management of their classrooms and need to retain final decisions about plans for change. As key components of the classroom ecological system, teachers have an insight into crucial classroom dynamics that can frame any interpretation of classroom data. Moreover, prior research has clearly established that teachers prefer collaborative consultants to expert ones (Pryzwansky & White, 1983).

STEP 2: GATHERING CLASSROOM DATA

In Step 2, the consultant collects data about the classroom characteristics. When ClassMaps surveys are used to collect classroom data, they require approximately 20–

25 minutes for a class to complete. In our work with classrooms, because some survey questions asked about the teacher or teaching practices, a team member who was not the teacher routinely read these to the class while the teacher worked in some other part of the classroom. Since reading levels vary widely, even within upper elementary and middle school classrooms, we routinely used an overhead projector to display surveys to the class, pointed to each item as it was read, and read each item twice. Another adult circulated around the room to make sure that students completed the surveys correctly.

Students have taught us the importance of explaining why the classroom data are being collected and how the information will be used. For example, one seventh grader asked, "Is this all about fixing our school? Because, if we knew that before we answered the questions, I think we would tell the truth." Since then, the instructions for the ClassMaps surveys have incorporated an example from another classroom where survey information was used to plan for classroom changes. The verbatim instructions that we used are included in Chapter 5.

STEP 3: ANALYZING AND GRAPHING THE DATA

In our model for classroom consultation, it is the consultant's task to analyze and graph the classroom data in a way that is easy for teachers and students to review and understand. Because classroom graphs will almost always be shown to students, their format needs to be clear, simple, and easy to interpret. For example, ClassMaps graphs are easiest for students to understand if each question's responses are described with simple bar graphs that show the number of students giving each response. In secondary classrooms, the graphs might instead show the percentage of students giving each response. (Additional information about data analysis and graphing can be found in Chapters 5 and 7.) Data graphs should always be carefully screened to ensure that there is no identifying information, such as the teacher's name or room number, that would identify the data should they be misplaced. In our work with classrooms, we generally ask teachers to choose a nonsense name that can be used to label their information without revealing their identity (e.g., Popeye, Magnum, or Queen Bee.)

STEP 4: SETTING A CLASSROOM GOAL

In step 4, the teacher and the classroom team examine the data and use it to set a goal for classroom change. If this is the first time that the team has met as a group, they will need some time to explore their common task. To start this process, each team member can explain his or her reasons for agreeing to be on the team and hear what has taken place before the current meeting.

The consultant who brings the graphs to the team may have the most experience in interpreting data and frequently has some tentative interpretations or interesting contrasts to point out to the team. However, if the team is to remain truly collaborative, this prior knowledge cannot be allowed to dominate the discussion. Good consultation practice recommends that interpretations be offered tentatively (Conoley & Conoley, 1992). Then, all team members can participate equally in decision making, work toward a common goal, and share accountability for outcomes (Friend & Cook, 1997). It is useful for the consultant to guide team meetings with process-oriented questions that prompt the team to discuss what each will contribute to the work of the team and what the goal of the team's work will be (Erchul, 1987). The Goal-Setting Worksheet found in Appendix B will enable the consultant to guide the team's process without the appearance of controlling the meeting.

A principal task in step 4 is to review the data graphs and identify the classroom strengths and weaknesses they reveal. This is a complicated process, and it can flow more smoothly if the consultant previews the worksheet to plan for future decisions and pencils in those decisions that have already been made. The questions constitute a functional analysis of the conditions under which the classroom weaknesses are evident and the features of the environment that might be supporting them. Although the consultant may ask other questions in addition to those on the worksheet, each question on the worksheet should be introduced in the order shown there, since they systematically lead the team to the ultimate decision—setting a goal for the classroom. It is very important that the team carefully consider the nature of those weaknesses and come to a common definition of them before planning classroom change.

Care should be taken to focus on positive features of the classroom as well as on problems and to present the classroom as a system with multiple elements that contribute to the learning climate. This systems focus will deter the team from viewing the graphs as a measure of the teacher's competence in leading the class. Two studies of solution-focused brief therapy (Metcalf, 1995; Walter & Peller, 1992) describe other ways to keep the focus positive and facilitate clear goal formulation. For example, asking when a given weakness is *not* present or is *not* a problem can describe conditions that could contribute to a successful solution for the weakness. The classroom's goal can be specified more clearly by asking the team members to describe in detail what they expect to see and not see when the weakness is no longer a concern in the classroom.

Step 4 concludes with the articulation of a goal for classroom change. This goal should be stated in language that is so clear and precise that everyone will be able to tell when the goal is met. Stating the goal inevitably identifies other data (frequency counts or student self-monitoring) that could be available in the classroom to mark progress toward the goal and identify when it is met. It is important to have at least 2 weeks of consistently collected data before the intervention plan is implemented, so baseline collection of these data should begin immediately following this goal-setting meeting. Consultants should make sure that data collection is as effortless and reliable as possible. Together with the ClassMaps surveys, these data constitute the baseline against which postintervention data will be compared to judge progress of the intervention. Finally, the consultant should verify that all team members know what tasks they are assigned over the next 2 weeks, identify a time for the classroom meeting (step 5), and schedule the next team meetings.

STEP 5: DISCUSSING CLASSROOM DATA WITH THE STUDENTS

Student participation is essential to ecological classroom change, because the system's multiple participants must share responsibility for intervention in order for changes to be meaningful and large. Consequently, in step 5, the teacher and consultant convene a classroom meeting to discuss classroom data with the students. The meeting gives students an opportunity to comment on the accuracy of the classroom data, explain their hypotheses for why weaknesses exist, and suggest strategies for change. To emphasize the students' shared responsibility for classroom change, they are specifically asked to identify things that they could do to make things better in addition to describing what they think the teacher could do.

Comprehensive instructions for conducting classroom meetings are described in Chapter 7, and a Classroom Meeting Worksheet is provided in Appendix B. A good strategy is for the consultant to lead the meeting while leaving a copy of the worksheet with the classroom teacher to keep the notes. The worksheet's questions should not constrict the class discussion. Instead it should proceed normally and comfortably. However, if each of the worksheet's questions are introduced in turn, all key meeting topics will be covered. One copy of the worksheet should be left with the teacher and another with the consultant so that both have copies of the class meeting notes.

STEP 6: MAKING A PLAN FOR CHANGE

By step 6, the classroom team will have collected multiple perspectives and ideas about why the classroom weaknesses have occurred and what can be done about them. In the step 6 team meeting, the team will write a plan for intervention, commit team members to carrying it out, and arrange for the collection of intervention data. The Intervention Planning Worksheet in Appendix B can serve as a guide for this discussion.

To develop the plan, the classroom team will first examine and interpret any additional classroom data that have been collected since the goal-setting meeting. The new data will refine the team's understanding of the weaknesses and clarify the conditions under which they present a problem for the class. This will lead naturally into a discussion of what else in the class contributes to these weaknesses, and to the formation of a hypothesis (an educated guess) about why they have emerged. This hypothesis is critical because it will guide the plan for classroom change.

Teachers play a central role in forming the hypothesis and plan, and it is crucial that the team remain sensitive to the personal responsibility that the teacher holds for the classroom's health and security. Sometimes a teacher's understanding of a classroom's weaknesses is complicated by emotion-laden themes that seem out of proportion to the problem. This lack of professional objectivity may cause the teacher to "catastrophize" the problem, and other team members may be tempted to buy into this negative perspective (Caplan, 1963). To restore objectivity, consultants can describe more reasonable and likely alternatives than the teacher's worst-case scenario without disputing the teacher's basic description of the problem (Caplan, 1970). Alternatively, the intervention plan can reflect the teacher's strongly held ideas as long as its impact is benign. Subsequent careful data collection will provide the needed objectivity to make corrections in the plan.

There are three principles that guide the design of an intervention plan. The first, *equifinality* (Katz & Kahn, 1978), means simply that there are many ways to achieve the same outcome. Teams should be encouraged to explore several alternative interventions before choosing one. This brainstorming may prompt the team to identify resources that would have gone unnoticed otherwise. Some teams may want the consultant to act as an expert and propose the "correct" intervention to them. However, a wise consultant will take a collaborative stance, adding to the intervention suggestions tentatively without displacing other team members' ideas and encouraging discussion so that an idea is not selected prematurely. A second principle is that a match must exist between the teacher's skill and the demands that a specific intervention might place on a class (Gresham, 1989). Some interventions can be adapted or changed without impacting their effectiveness, whereas others cannot. Consultants should prompt teams to anticipate what might go wrong with an intervention, whether it needs to be altered to match classroom resources, and whether it will still be effective if altered. Finally, the acceptability of the intervention to the teacher should be considered (Elliott, 1988). Interventions will be more acceptable if they are described in language that matches the teacher's perspective on the problem (Conoley, Conoley, Ivey, & Scheel, 1991) and the classroom's cultural values (Brown, Pryzwansky, & Schulte, 2001). Teachers will accept and implement interventions if they expect that they will be able to do so effectively and if they are rewarded for their efforts by outcomes they value (Tollefson, 2000).

It is important that the classroom interventions balance empirical rigor with pragmatism. Consequently, we have identified two levels of interventions for teams to select from. First, informal interventions have been identified for each classroom characteristic; these were included as recommendations by researchers investigating each characteristic. For example, an informal intervention to enhance peer relationships in a classroom is to increase the students' opportunities to engage in enjoyable learning activities within pairs or small groups. The effectiveness of this intervention is suggested by Logan and colleagues' (1997) research on cooperative learning in general education classrooms and Berndt's (1999) research on the impact of friendships on academic learning. Classroom teams will generally select from these informal interventions first because they are easier and faster to implement. However, when classroom data show that these informal interventions have not been effective, evidence-based interventions have also been identified to enhance each classroom characteristic. These are interventions with formal intervention manuals that have been demonstrated in well-controlled studies to enhance one or more of the classroom characteristics. Although they require more effort and discipline to implement, they can be effective in situations that require substantial change. Chapter 8 describes both informal and evidenced-based interventions for the six classroom characteristics.

At the end of the step 6 team meeting, there needs to be a written plan for intervention that describes each action to be taken, the person responsible for it, and when it will occur. A Plan Record Worksheet is included in Appendix B. It breaks the plan into a step-by-step sequence and can record each team member's commitments.

Step 6 concludes by revisiting the plan for data collection. Data collection during intervention should remain consistent with the way data were collected at the baseline so that new data can be compared to baseline data. Data collected from this point forward will be used to determine whether or not the class is successfully reaching its goal or how to modify the plan so that the goal is met.

STEP 7: INTERVENTION

Two important tasks need to be accomplished in step 7. First, the intervention activities need to be carried out as planned. The best intervention plans are simple so that the classroom is not overwhelmed with too many changes at one time. Plans that are very complex can be implemented in steps, making the easiest changes and those that are expected to have the greatest impact first. Some teachers will want the consultant to provide direct help with plan implementation. This help can take the form of modeling some of the activities that another team member will eventually take over or working directly with students in large or small groups. Like any other team members, consultants should not make time commitments they cannot reasonably keep. Intervention plans that demand too much of a team will need to be revised, or responsibility for implementation should be shared with others in addition to the core team. Moreover, intervention plans that are too complex will be difficult to incorporate into the regular classroom routines.

The integrity of the implementation is especially important, since most plans that fail do so because they were never truly implemented. A common error is to expect team members to carry out activities with which they have little or no experience (Gresham, 1989). To guard against unintended deviations, the consultant should check with the teacher at least once a week to review data and monitor the progress of the plan. In some cases, teachers have a good reason to deviate from a plan. Careful record keeping can identify aspects of the plan that were difficult to implement, focus efforts to revise the plan as needed, and ultimately lead to greater acceptance and use of the plan over time. The Plan Record Worksheet in Appendix B can be used to track plan implementation. The simple "Yes–Partly–No" format allows quick review of each component of the plan and also serves to remind the team of the plan's key steps. In some cases, it will be useful to pull the team back together to consider alternative plans. Effective consultants will reconvene the team to revise the plan when this is necessary, but they do not revise it too quickly. Any plan of action needs a sufficient trial period, usually 2 weeks, before its effectiveness can be determined.

Some classroom teachers will appreciate the data and intervention ideas but will want to develop and work on interventions themselves without team support. Still others may implement the plan for a time, then change it without informing the consultant or the team. A challenge in step 7 will be to maintain the team's commitment to the plan as written and to make modifications in systematic and thoughtful ways.

STEP 8: MONITORING THE PLAN

A critical step in classroom intervention is to monitor the progress of the plan in meeting the classroom's goal. Toward this end, the classroom team should collect continuous classroom data relevant to the goal and the consultant should analyze and monitor the data to determine whether or not progress is evident and whether the goal has been met. In some cases, the classroom plan will work quickly and efficiently, sometimes in less than a month. At that point, the consultant can collate the classroom data and reconvene the classroom's team one last time for debriefing and to plan for routinizing the intervention into ongoing classroom practices. Routinization is different from the "generalization" that completes individual change programs. Generalization is intended to instate students' target behaviors in diverse situations while fading the artificial consequences imposed by the intervention. In classroom change programs, the goal is not to fade the supports for learning that have been introduced into the classroom, but rather to embed them into the classroom's ongoing routines and practices even after the project has ended. A final meeting should also be held with the students to share the data and celebrate their collective success.

In other cases, the classroom's plan will not appear to be working or only some parts of it will be working. In this case, the team should return to step 5 and consider making revisions to the plan or goal. When interventions are not effective, it may be because the "dosage" of the intervention was insufficient. That is, the intervention activities may be appropriate but may need to happen more often or for longer periods of time. Alternatively, it is possible that the intervention was not implemented with integrity and that the activities strayed so far from the original intervention plan that it was never truly provided to the classroom. In some cases, the classroom may need to institute a more rigorous intervention, drawing from an evidenced-based intervention whose effectiveness has been documented in the research literature. Finally, it is possible that the original functional analysis of the classroom's learning context was inaccurate or overlooked key information. At any point where an intervention plan is being revised, it is also wise to review and refine classroom data collection procedures to be consistent, objective, and comprehensive.

In still other cases, the class will reach its first goal and decide to redirect attention to a second goal. When this happens, it is recommended that comprehensive classroom data be re-collected, since progress on one goal can affect the profile of the class in other areas. The same team can remain, or a new team can be convened and the process begun again.

A CONSULTATION EXAMPLE

Ellie, a third-grade teacher, sought consultation with the school psychologist because she was finding it difficult to interact comfortably with her "very needy group of students." She explained that the students acted "very mean to each other" and frequently argued with her and the classroom aide. She had implemented classroom meetings in an attempt to address these behaviors but was frustrated because the problems didn't seem to be decreasing.

The consultant suggested that a team problem-solving approach could help with her concerns, and together they invited the classroom aide and another third-grade teacher to join them. During the first team meeting, when asked to describe the most important problem to address, Ellie responded, "We need to ask the students . . . they know best." The consultant offered to collect anonymous surveys to reveal the classroom's most pressing concerns and to provide visual feedback to the team.

The consultant graphed the survey results and brought the graphs along with the Goal-Setting Worksheet (Figure 6.1) to a team meeting. As the team discussed the graphs, the consultant completed the worksheet. Ellie expressed dismay at the number of students who responded "Sometimes" or "No" to questions on the teacher–student relationships survey (shown in Figure 6.2). She explained that at the beginning of the school year she had felt so pressured to cover a lot material and bring up sagging test scores that she might have overlooked the importance of establishing rapport and listening carefully to her students. She wondered if her students' perception that they lacked rapport with her could also be affecting their relationships with each other. This led her to a goal for the classroom: to improve her relationship with her students to see if their relationships with each other also improved.

When the consultant showed the teacher–student relationships graph to Ellie's class a few days later, the students agreed that they would like to have a better relationship with their teacher and that the class would also be more enjoyable if they got along with each other better. They came up with the idea of making "friendship bracelets" for each other out of colored string to remind themselves to treat each other like friends rather than people they didn't care about. They also agreed to make sure that everyone was included equally during group activities. The consultant supported their idea and led them in a discussion of how friends treat each other and resolve conflicts.

GOAL-SETTING WORKSHEET

Classroom: *Ellie's third grade* Date of goal setting: *January 29*

What strengths are shown by your classroom data?

Most kids in the class have someone to eat with at lunch. The students are talking to their parents about school. They're asking for help when they need it.

What weaknesses are shown that you would like to see improve?

Lots of students respond "Sometimes" or "No" when talking about the teacher relationship. There is a lot of peer conflict reported. Students describe lots of disruptive behavior in the class.

Which of these weaknesses is the most important one to change?

The relationship between the teacher and students.

In addition to the classroom data, what other evidence do you have that this weakness is a problem for the class?

There are frequent arguments between the students and the teacher and aide. Students are mean to each other.

What are the times and places when this weakness is particularly a problem for the class?

Before and after school. As students come in from lunch recess. During reading groups. When the seatwork is difficult.

What are the times and places when this weakness is not present or is not a problem for the class?

When I'm having "special lunch" with the students. During times of direct instruction.

What else is happening in the class that might be contributing to this weakness? (Examples might include certain individuals who are present, the size of the group, time of day, seating arrangement, expectations for a task, and the degree of structure or last of structure present.)

There's a lot of emphasis on catching up with academic standards—these kids were behind at the end of last year. These kids are pretty competitive with each other.

FIGURE 6.1. Example of a completed Goal-Setting Worksheet.

What will the classroom be like once the weakness is "fixed"? This will be the **Classroom Goal**.

Students will be courteous to the teacher and to each other.

How will you know if your class meets the goal?

Teacher's daily notes will show fewer student arguments in class.

Students will describe a more positive teacher relationship.

There will be fewer arguments at recess.

What additional data will you collect for your classroom goal?

What data will be collected? *Daily teacher notes of arguments (1) in class and (2) at recess.*

Who will collect the data? *Ellie.*

When and how often? *Each day immediately after recess.*

Plan for your class meeting

What classroom data would you like to show to the class? (Consider showing one graph reflecting a class strength and a second graph reflecting a class weakness.)

The teacher–student relationships graph.

What questions do you want to ask the class about the data?

- ☑ Does the class think the data are accurate?
- ☑ What do they think the teacher could do differently to make things better?
- ☑ What do they think the students could do to make things better?
- ☑ What else might help make things better?
- ☐ Other questions? *None.*

When should the team meet again?

(By then, the class meeting will have been held, there will be more data, and the team can discuss a plan for class change.)
A good time and date: *February 5 after school.*

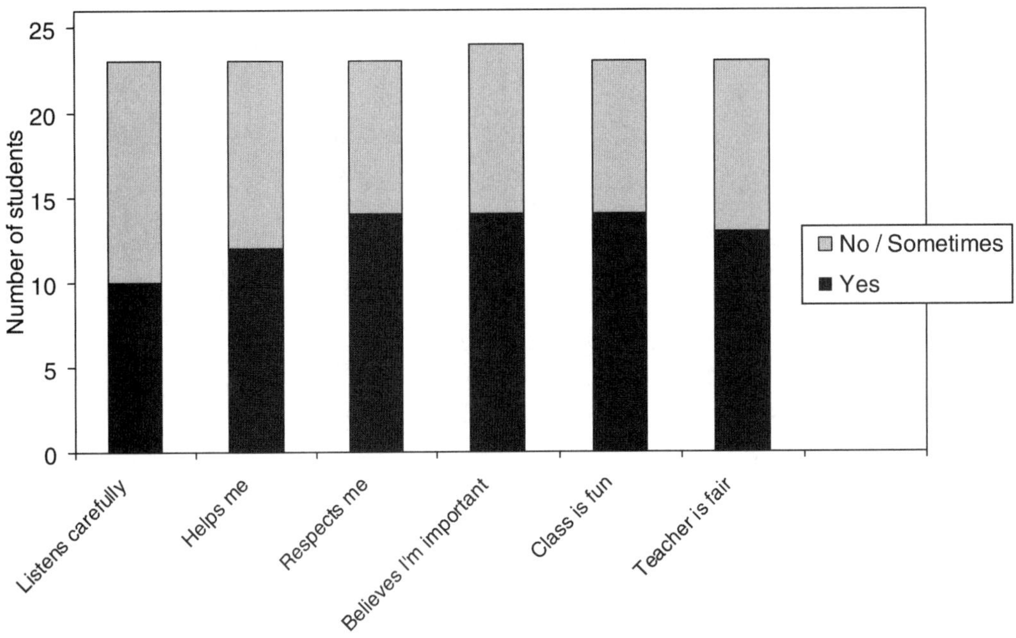

FIGURE 6.2. Teacher–student relationships graph.

Ellie kept notes on the Classroom Meeting Worksheet (Figure 6.3), and as she listened she felt that she was on the right track.

Next, Ellie's team met to plan a classroom intervention to achieve the goal. Using the solution-focused approach (Metcalf, 1995), the consultant asked Ellie to describe the things that were going well in her relations with students. She replied that she often had lunch with the students who were well behaved and finished their work. She commented that she'd never really considered spending "special" time with the students whose behavior was not up to her standards. When the consultant asked if she might consider doing that, Ellie commented, "Looking at these graphs, it's like a light bulb going off in my head. Of course the struggling students need extra attention—probably more than the kids who are doing well. I should have been paying more attention to that all year."

Continuing the solution-focused approach, the consultant asked if there was anything Ellie could think of doing now to begin turning things around. Ellie commented, "I need to stop looking at giving special time to students as a reward and start thinking of it as a good teaching strategy. After all, I give them extra help when they're having a hard time with math or writing!" This comment led to a discussion among the team members about implementing the "banking time" intervention (Pianta, 1999; Pianta & Hamre, 2001) described more fully in Chapter 8. In banking time, the teacher spends special time with students doing an activity of their choice, thus strengthening the quality of the relationship. The consultant and the team completed the Plan Record Worksheet (Figure 6.4), specifying how and when Ellie would spend time with her

CLASSROOM MEETING WORKSHEET

Classroom: *Ellie's third grade* Date of class meeting: *February 3*

What questions were asked of the class?

- ☑ Do you think the classroom data are accurate?
- ☑ What do you think caused the problem?
- ☑ What do you think the teacher could do differently to make things better?
- ☑ What do you think students could do to make things better?

Did the class think that the classroom data were accurate?

- ☐ Completely inaccurate
- ☐ Kind of inaccurate
- ☐ Neutral
- ☑ Accurate with a few inaccuracies
- ☐ Very accurate

What words did the class use to describe the problem?

Kids are mean. We're grumpy most of the time. This is a grouchy classroom.

What did the students think caused the problem?

Sometimes we have a bad day at home. We give our teacher a headache a lot. Kids copy what they see in other classes. We forget that we like each other. Sometimes other kids won't let you play.

What did the students think they could do to make things better?

Put up posters to remind each other to be nice.

Just think carefully before you say something mean.

Wear friendship bracelets to remind us to be nice.

Play games that everyone can play.

What did the students think the teacher could do to make things better?

Remind us to be nice.

Make us stay inside if we forget to let other kids play.

Be nicer.

Take an aspirin for her headache.

Play more fun games and have more fun times in class.

My dad meditates when he gets too grouchy.

FIGURE 6.3. Example of a completed Classroom Meeting Worksheet.

PLAN RECORD WORKSHEET

Classroom: *Ellie's third grade* Record for week of: ____________________

	Did this happen?
Activity 1 What will be done? *Take turns giving "special time" at lunch to the three kids that are struggling most: Matthew, Lisette, Arnie.* Who will do it? *Ellie.* When? *Every Tuesday and Thursday at lunch period.* Where? *In the classroom.*	YES PARTLY NO
Activity 2 What will be done? *Plan a fun learning game for the mid-morning break.* Who will do it? *Ellie and the class.* When? *Every day from 10 to 10:20 a.m.* Where? *In the classroom.*	YES PARTLY NO
Activity 3 What will be done? *Make friendship bracelets to remind us to be kind to classmates.* Who will do it? *Classroom students.* When? *Week 1.* Where? *In the classroom.*	YES PARTLY NO

FIGURE 6.4. Example of a completed Plan Record Worksheet.

FIGURE 6.4 *(continued)*

What data will be collected? *Daily teacher notes of arguments (1) in class and (2) at recess.*

Who will collect the data? *Ellie.*

When and how often? *Each day immediately after recess.*

How will the information be recorded? *A count of the number of arguments teacher had with kids, number of arguments aide had with kids, number of arguments kids had with each other in class, and number of arguments kids had with each other at recess.*

Use this chart to record data as appropriate.

	Monday	Tuesday	Wednesday	Thursday	Friday
With teacher					
With aide					
Kids in class					
Kids outside					

What did the data show?

____

____

____

Attach the actual data records.

troubled students individually and with the class as a group, and how data to evaluate the intervention would be collected.

The consultation process yielded many benefits for Ellie and the students in her classroom. She gained increased awareness of her students' social–emotional needs and of her own ability to support troubled students. She was able to reframe her construct of "good teaching" to include providing special time and attention to students as they needed it. She no longer perceived the extra attention as "rewarding bad behavior" but as an effective teaching strategy to build positive relationships between herself and at-risk students. Several months into the consultation process, Ellie reported that other teachers in the building were eager to hear about her new strategies and wanted anonymous surveys administered in their classrooms. Ellie's new-found role of an in-house professional development resource provided her with an increased sense of teaching efficacy and optimism for the start of the next school year.

SUMMARY

This chapter has described data-based consultation procedures that will be familiar to anyone who has worked on a school's student assistance teams, but classroom change rather than student change has been made the focus of the process. The ultimate purpose of this classroom consultation is to design, implement, and assess the impact of classroom interventions to improve the learning supports for students. Chapter 7 follows up on this discussion by providing a further explanation of ways that students can be more fully involved in the intervention process, and Chapter 8 describes alternative intervention strategies that classroom teams might use.

ANNOTATED BIBLIOGRAPHY

Dinkmeyer, D., & Carlson, J. (2001). *Consultation: Creating school-based interventions.* Ann Arbor, MI: Sheridan Books.

Dinkmeyer and Carlson assert that direct intervention with one student at a time is fast becoming a luxury that research does not support. They believe a paradigm shift is occurring among school mental health professionals: where they once worked directly with individual students, they are now focused on modifying the contextual aspects of classrooms and schools. When consultants view students with problems as living within unhealthy families, classrooms, or schools, they can work with teachers and parents to develop goal-directed interventions that build on existing strengths. School mental health professionals should promote egalitarian relationships with consultees that are trusting, respectful, and facilitative of the consultees' potential to solve problems. Based upon humanistic and Adlerian psychology, the authors provide practical guidelines for effective consultation and numerous examples of effective classroom-based strategies for change.

Ingraham, C. L. (2000). Consultation through a multicultural lens: Multicultural and cross-cultural consultation in schools. *School Psychology Review, 29*, 320–343.

This special issue of *School Psychology Review* is devoted to multicultural and cross-cultural consultation and contains articles that are critical reading for any school mental health professional. The Ingraham article presents a multicultural school consultation (MSC) framework that is highly accessible and immediately relevant to the school-based practitioner. The MSC framework is an approach in which cultural issues are raised and adjustments to traditional consultation models are made. With a sensitive and dynamic style, cultural variations in the consultation constellation are illuminated that involve the many cultural triads within which school mental health consultants will inevitably operate. Practical consultation strategies are provided that will assist practitioners when working with consultees and clients when either or both are from different cultural backgrounds. Practitioners of all cultural backgrounds will appreciate this coherent articulation of multicultural dynamics and the professional development needs that exist for new practitioners and veterans alike.

Metcalf, L. (1995). *Counseling toward solutions: A practical solution-focused program for working with students, teachers, and parents.* West Nyack, NY: Center for Applied Research in Education.

This book is a valuable resource for the novice or the seasoned school mental health professional interested in learning about solution-focused brief therapy in school settings. In a clear, well-organized, and entertaining way, Metcalf explains that a focus on solutions capitalizes on the fact that no problem occurs all the time. Rather than seeking to eliminate problems through an examination of why they occur, the solution to most problems can be found in the exceptions when they are absent—because a problem is not a problem when it is not occurring! Metcalf provides multiple case examples and dialogues to illustrate how our thinking and language need to change in order to stop focusing on problems and start focusing on competencies. She gives examples of how to apply such solution-focused standards as the miracle question, scaling questions, search for exceptions, and goal setting to work with students in a counseling session and with teachers and parents in a consultation setting. Also included are numerous worksheets to support solution-focused efforts. Also by the same author and publisher is *Teaching Toward Solutions: Step-by-Step Strategies for Handling Academic, Behavior and Family Issues in the Classroom* (1999). The latter book is full of ideas that consultants can use with consultees who want to change their own behavior in ways that facilitate change in others.

Parsons, R. D. (1996). *The skilled consultant: A systematic approach to the theory and practice of consultation.* Needham Heights, MA: Simon & Schuster.

Parsons asserts that success in school-based consultation requires a sensitive balance between consultation techniques, on the one hand, and the orientation and values of the consultant, on the other. Successful consultants are highly attuned to the relational and contextual aspects of the environments in which they work and appreciate the impact of school, community, and environmental factors in children's problems. Consultation has the broadest impact on students when it leads to the modification of processes and structures within which a school operates. The book discusses numerous strategies for promoting effective consultation relationships, helps practitioners understand consultee resistance as a natural developmental phenomenon, and provides practical strategies for ameliorating resistance and equalizing any real or perceived power differentials. Solutions that improve the skills of the consultee, so that fixed problems stay fixed, are emphasized. A wealth of realistic case examples and review exercises helps bring the material to life.

7

Including the Classroom's Students in Planning and Decision Making

Thus far, this book has described six essential characteristics of resilient classrooms, the tools and methods that can be used to assess these characteristics, and a framework for fostering classroom change. This chapter describes the strategies for engaging the classroom's students in interpreting their classroom's data, setting goals for classroom change, and acting as agents of change within their classroom. Much of this work will be initiated within the context of classroom meetings, with students taking responsibility for following through on the plans that are made during those meetings.

The collaborative discovery orientation of classroom meetings is very similar to student-centered constructivist teaching. The process is cocrafted with students whose spontaneous ideas may be very different from those that adults had anticipated. Still, classroom meetings are planned and coordinated, rigorous events that include specific steps so that the necessary information is gathered and require skilled facilitation so that all class members can participate comfortably and readily. Classroom meetings also require a high degree of focused energy from the facilitators, who are responsible for monitoring both the meetings' content and the process for accuracy and sensitivity. Finally, classroom meetings require flexibility, since the methods and strategies must vary to accommodate individual differences in classrooms and their members. Discussion strategies need to be adjusted to the concerns and purposes of each meeting, and these can change over time even within the same classroom.

This chapter describes a collaborative process for conducting classroom meetings that relies upon students and teachers to identify the characteristics of their classroom that need to be enhanced and the methods that will facilitate those changes. Four things generally happen during these meetings: first, data describing the classroom characteristics are presented to students; second, discussions explore student interpretations of the data; third, students make suggestions for ways to change the classroom that may subsequently be incorporated into the classroom's intervention plan; and, fourth, students are assigned responsibilities for implementing the intervention. Inevitably, as the plan is carried out, revisions are required and it becomes necessary to evaluate how well the intervention is working. Consequently, follow-up classroom meetings must be convened so that students can participate in these decisions as well. To describe these meetings clearly, a classroom example is provided at the end of this chapter. Above all else, student participation is most active and useful when students know that their ideas are taken seriously and their suggestions probably will be used.

The classroom meeting process described in this chapter is derived from the numerous approaches to facilitating classroom meetings (Developmental Studies Center, 1996; Glasser, 1969; P. S. Murphy, 2002). A few key rules govern their effective facilitation. It is important that facilitators ask questions, listen carefully, and confirm what they have heard with students to be certain that they understand how students are feeling about classroom life. This requires that the facilitator be an alert and respectful partner in the inquiry process and follows the lead from students and teachers. In turn, this leads to greater student and teacher engagement in the process. It is also important that the teacher not be the primary facilitator of the classroom's meeting. Teachers play a critical role in determining the classroom characteristics and need to be able to participate freely in discussions about the classroom's data and plans for change. This gives students the implicit message that the teacher is working with them to plan for change, rather than imposing changes on them. Facilitation responsibilities can be difficult for teachers to juggle simultaneously with this participation. Finally, the social climate that is created within classroom meetings inevitably spills over into other classroom activities, so it is critical that these meetings strengthen the respect that students have for their teacher and each other.

PRESENTING CLASSROOM DATA TO STUDENTS

In resilient classroom meetings, students are shown data about their classroom's characteristics to prompt their planning and guide their decision making. Initially, adults should decide which pieces of the data should be shared with students. Large amounts of data can confuse students and make it difficult for them to draw out meaningful interpretations. Next, a diagram or graph of the data can be prepared. Visual displays of data make it easier for students to see the relevance of the data and to estimate the size and importance of differences and trends. These graphs are most effective when they first present the "big picture" to students and then proceed to finer details. As a rule, students can integrate the key points most easily when fewer, more important facts are provided.

Presentation of these graphs and charts usually is the initiating event in a resilient classroom meeting. An overhead of the diagram is displayed at the front of the group and the strengths and weaknesses shown in the data are described briefly. Sometimes the discussion of the classroom data may require "stirring the pot" a little. The facilitator may point out apparent contradictions in the data or generate student interest in subtle aspects of the data.

Examples of data charts and graphs that we have used are distributed throughout this book. However, in the early elementary grades, it is sometimes necessary to simplify graphs even further. For example, data diagrams can be restricted to one or two critical pieces of data displayed in a clear, engaging format. Figures 7.1 and 7.2 show two different graphs from a ClassMaps survey for academic self-determination. Figure 7.1 is an illustrated chart that described two important pieces of information for a second-grade urban classroom. Figure 7.2 is a six-bar graph that describes the same kind of information for an eighth-grade class. The simplified chart used with second graders conveyed very similar information, but its format allowed the younger students to understand the data easily and move comfortably into problem solving.

Figure 7.3 shows a graph from a teacher–student relationships survey. A third-grade classroom's teacher believed that it would confuse her students, as the class had not yet started their graphing unit. Therefore, in Figure 7.4, the graph was simplified to show only the most important information that required student feedback and discussion. Having fewer bars to focus on and using the "number of students" instead of

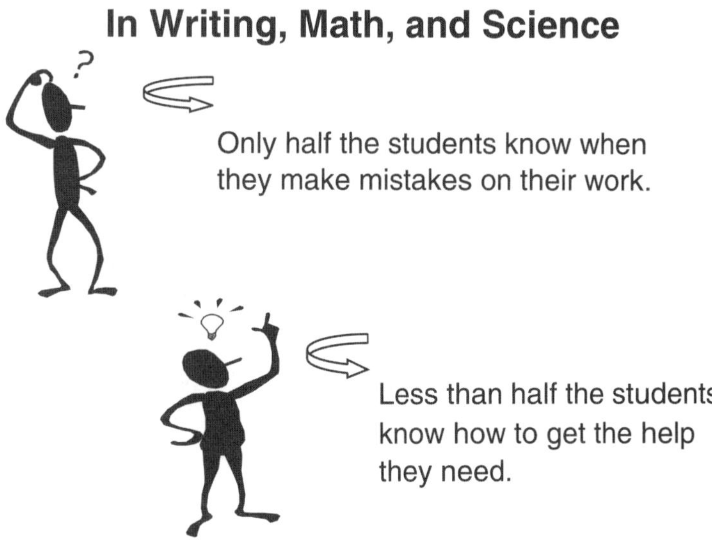

FIGURE 7.1. Early elementary example of a classroom's ClassMaps survey results for self-determination.

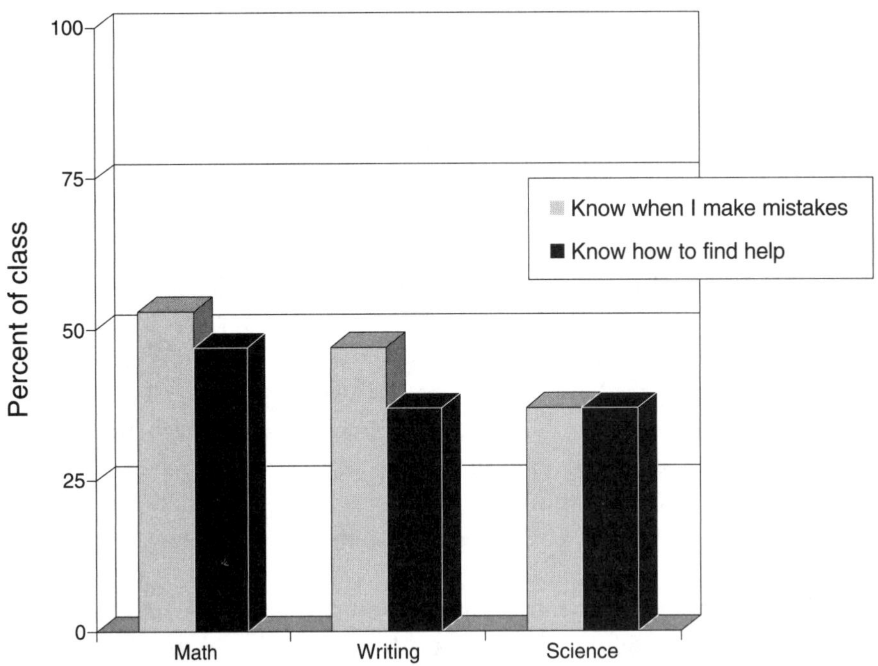

FIGURE 7.2. Middle school example of a classroom's ClassMaps survey results for self-determination.

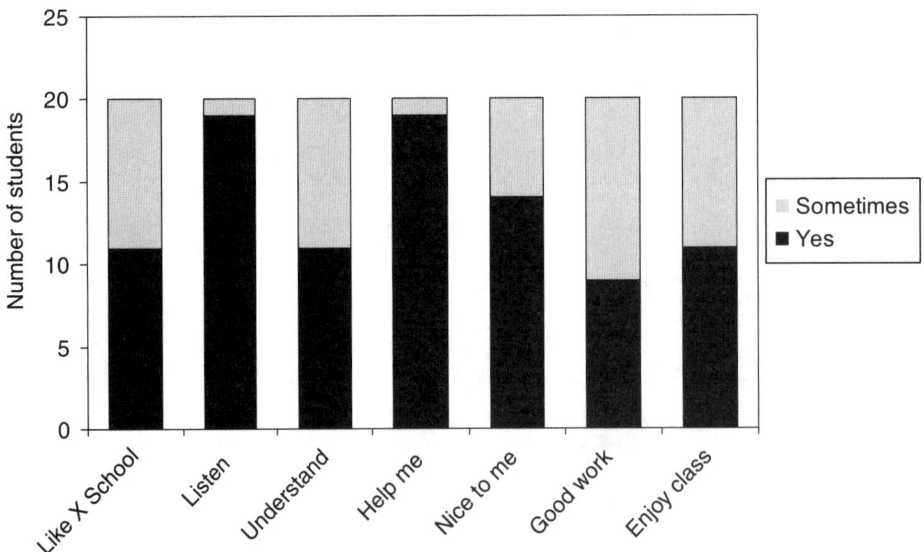

FIGURE 7.3. Complex example of a classroom's ClassMaps survey results for teacher–student relationships.

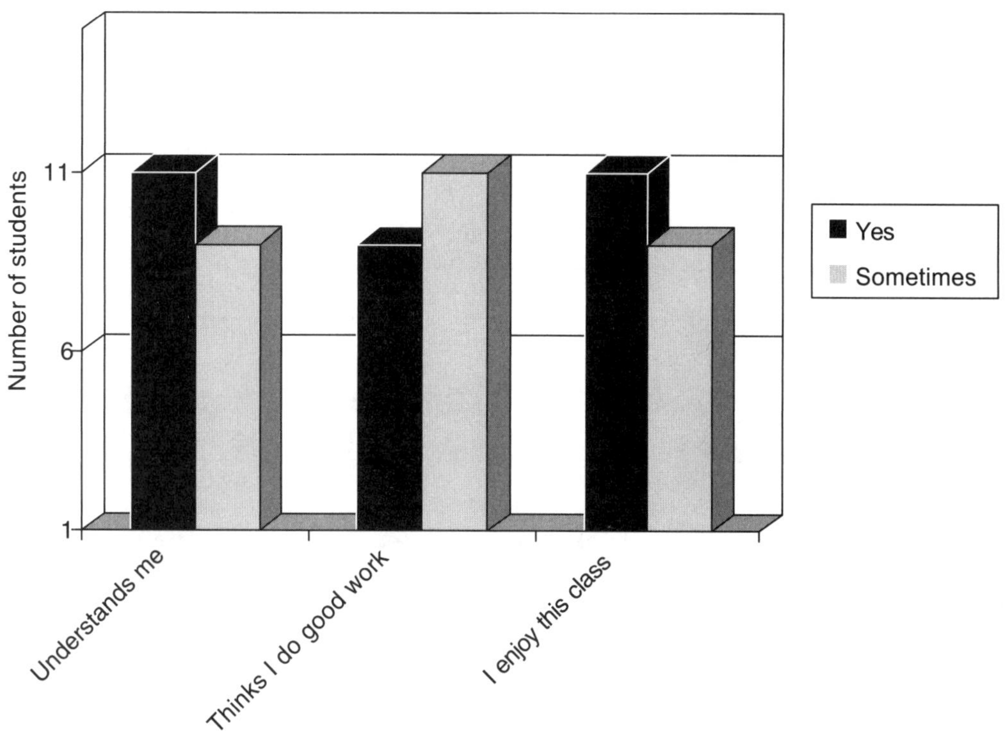

FIGURE 7.4. Simplified example of a classroom's ClassMaps survey results for teacher–student relationships.

"percentage of students" on the y-axis made it possible for students to interpret the data more easily.

Sociometric data can be more complicated than survey data, but they are easily simplified so that students can reflect upon and understand them. Figure 7.5 is part of a sociogram from a fifth-grade urban classroom that was performing well below the norm on state academic standards. This diagram was used to launch a weekly classroom intervention to improve the students' goal-setting skills. (This intervention is described in detail in Chapter 8.) This presentation of sociometric data helped students select their classroom's academic and social goals, and plan for ways to reach those goals. While the data described individual students strengths and weaknesses, they did not identify any students by name. The chart prompted a rich discussion about which student on the chart represented the "ideal" that classmates would like to emulate. Then, the conversation quickly expanded into a discussion about what made some classmates more socially effective than others.

Figure 7.6 shows a chart that was used to show sociometric data to a third–fourth-grade classroom that was struggling with significant peer conflicts and chronic behavior referrals. This simple visual summary of the data led to a productive conversation without the potential of deepening the conflict between any of the students.

	Student 1	Student 2	Student 3	Student 4	Student 5	Student 6
A lot of friends	4	12	1	4	3	1
Like to work with	5	6	0	3	3	0
Like to play with	7	7	1	2	3	1
Bugs kids most	0	0	5	1	1	6
Who finishes their work	6	5	1	2	2	0
Who often breaks the rules	1	0	6	1	2	4

FIGURE 7.5. Complex example of a classroom's sociometric rating survey results.

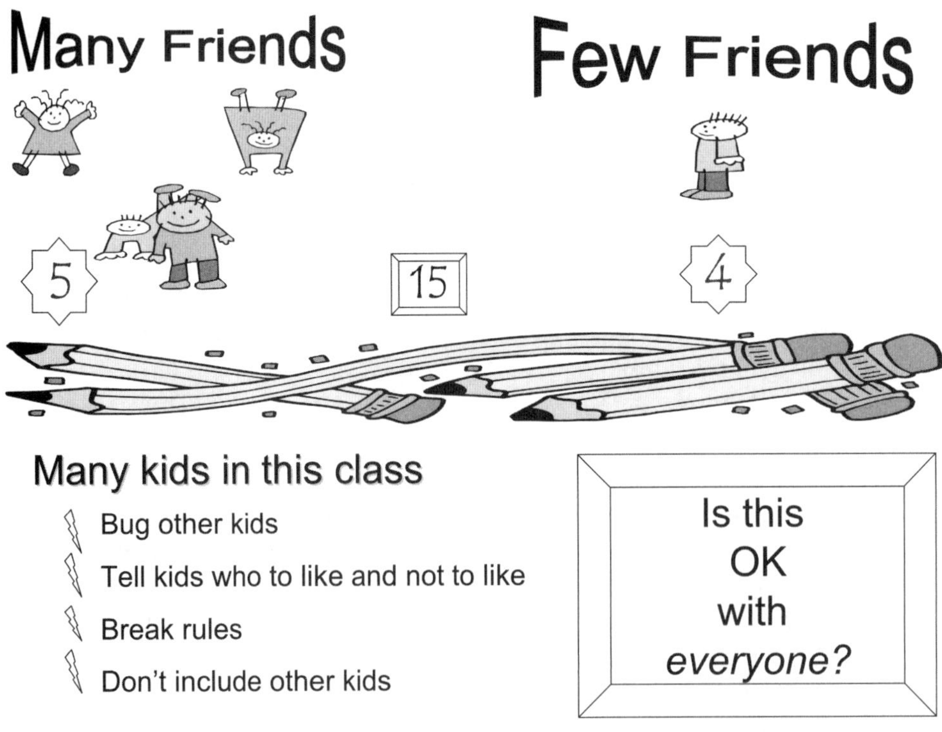

FIGURE 7.6. Simplified example of a classroom's sociometric rating survey results.

ENGAGING STUDENTS IN CLASSROOM MEETINGS

Discussion of the data's interpretation might well engage students' interest in a complex problem-solving discussion about the classroom. Students might be asked to describe the nature of the problem in their own words, to make guesses about why it is occurring in their classroom, to generate multiple recommendations for class change, and to suggest the recommendation that they believe will be most effective.

It is important to ask for student recommendations by first asking what the students could do differently to make things better and then what they think the teacher could do to help. Without this distinction, many students assume that the teacher is the only one who can make changes happen in their classroom. Problem-solving meetings are much more useful if students generate lots of recommendations for change. The most effective recommendations are often in the middle of a long list—not at the top where the more obvious recommendations reside, and not at the bottom once the class starts searching for a solution. Consequently, it is important to resist the temptation to prematurely move to intervention planning before all of the recommendations have been heard.

One person, often the teacher, should be responsible for keeping a written record of what the class says during the classroom meeting. (A sample Classroom Meeting Worksheet is available in Appendix B.) This record will ensure that unexpected and innovative ideas that the class contributes will not be lost during future planning.

There are a number of essential ingredients that increase the likelihood that students will participate actively in their classroom's meeting and contribute innovative ideas to the discussion. First, it is important to create a climate of "relaxed alertness" in the classroom (Caine & Caine, 1994). This term describes an optimal atmosphere for discussion in classrooms—a condition of high challenge and low threat. Second, a certain level of disequilibrium must be generated in the students. Students' thinking tends to be more productive and their contributions to be authentic when they are presented with challenging questions, unexpected data, or innovative ideas from each other. Since data usually provide fresh perspectives about the class, the presentation of data in resilient classroom meetings almost always cues high-quality student participation. Third, discussions generally are most spontaneous when students feel free to say what they think and respond honestly to the views of classmates and their teachers. Further, the social–emotional learning that can occur within these discussions may also contribute to students' understanding of themselves, their relationships, and their places in the classroom.

A classroom's data can guide the progress of each classroom meeting. No two classroom meetings are the same since classroom concerns vary markedly from one classroom to the next and within the same classroom across the year. Because the meetings make no assumptions about the "true" meaning of the data until the students have provided their interpretations, unanticipated interpretations can sometimes shift the focus of the conversation in interesting and very useful ways. For example, Figure 7.7 shows a graph of recess problems from a fifth-grade inner-city classroom.

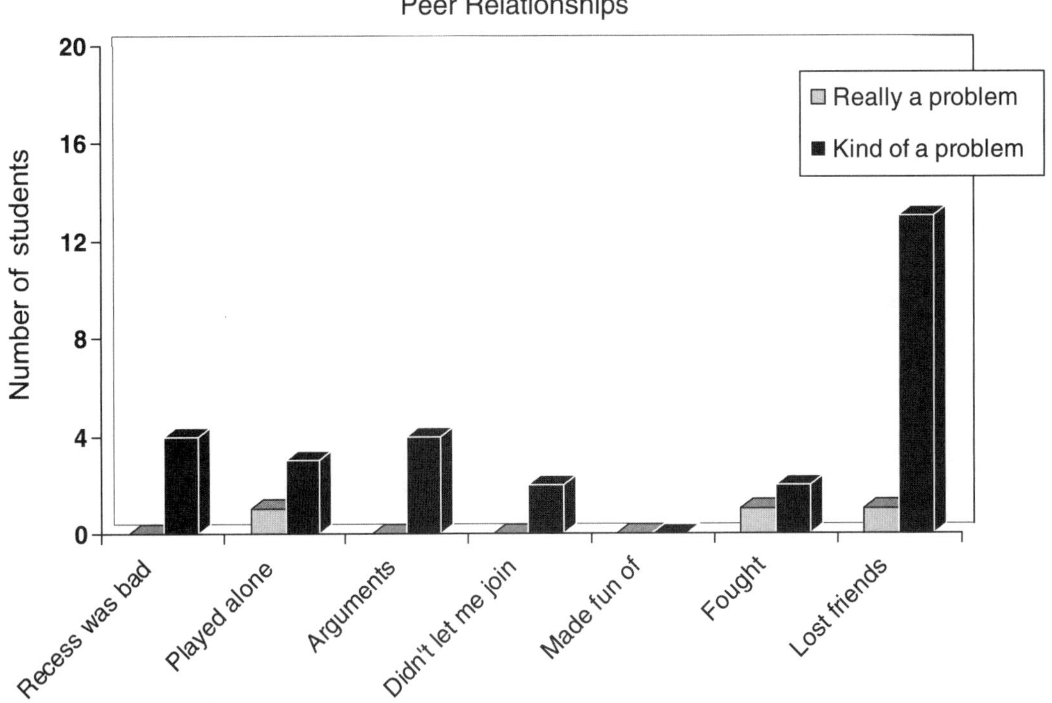

FIGURE 7.7. Example of a classroom's recess ratings for an atypical day.

This very positive assessment of the recess period suggests that there were no concerns about peer interactions in this class. Only a very few children reported problems with arguing or being made fun of, and not one student reported that recess was "bad." Nevertheless, students in this class said that this report described an atypical day, and that most of their recesses were fraught with arguments and lost friendships. Ultimately, the class planned an intervention to fix their recess problems because these were more pressing than any of the other issues presented in the meeting.

USING STUDENT SUGGESTIONS FOR CHANGE

The suggestions that students propose to answer complex problems are sometimes simplistic and shortsighted. Even then, elements in the suggestions can be incorporated into the classroom's cocrafted intervention. For example, a classroom was struggling with excess teasing and one student was convinced that enlarging the classroom's "no teasing" signs would help. While this was not an essential component of the intervention, it was included in the final plan because it would do no harm and would secure student commitment to the intervention. Using pieces of the students' suggestions in the plan for change validates their efforts and makes it more likely that they will buy into the final plan. Classroom interventions must be acceptable to all key participants at multiple levels of the classroom system so that the intervention can be implemented with integrity and enthusiasm.

Solution-focused counseling techniques (J. J. Murphy, 1997) can focus students' contributions to intervention planning so that they build on the classroom's prior successes. The technique provides ground rules that classrooms can fall back on when there are divergent opinions disrupting their discussion. For example, it is often helpful to speak of moving away from complaints about the status quo and toward more positive, proactive solutions. Solution-focused techniques also foster tolerance and acceptance by emphasizing that there are many paths to the same solution and that more than one student can be "right." Within this framework, the classroom learns that if something is working well, it makes sense to do more of it and that practices that are not working should be stopped. Minor changes are valued even if they will not solve the whole problem because small changes can lead to bigger ones. The students can be pulled more fully into the intervention activities once they notice and appreciate the improvements that occur from small changes. Solution-focused counseling also discourages the use of absolutes, because these are nonproductive and rarely accurate. For example, it's hard to agree to a student's suggestion that a bus driver be fired because he or she is "always" mean. At the same time, engaging the classroom in finding exceptions to absolutes is very productive. Most students can recall the bus driver being "nice" at least sometimes, and those occasions may become the seed that grows into an effective plan for better relationships with the bus driver.

MAKING STUDENTS PARTNERS IN INTERVENTION

Participation from a classroom's students can also simplify the complex task of implementing classroom interventions. Students can contribute to the work of collecting classroom data and graphing or analyzing the data. They can play key roles in implementing classroom interventions and in staffing the new tasks that an intervention might impose. For example, a second-grade class was temporarily housed in a sports arena while the school was undergoing asbestos removal, and the halogen lighting made it impossible to use overhead projectors to show the class data. Two students drew up a large copy of the classroom's data graph so that the class could discuss it together. A fifth-grade classroom was collecting daily surveys about recess problems as part of their classroom project to reduce playground conflicts. A student was assigned the task of collecting the surveys as the students came in from recess while the teacher prepared for the afternoon lesson. A fourth-grade class modified their lunchtime soccer game so that the rules were clear and were consistently enforced by the referee. Because playground aids were not available to referee the game, the class assigned students to that role and arranged for a "referee-training curriculum" to make sure that the students would be successful. Another fourth-grade class established problem-solving notes for students to complete when they were caught up in a conflict; the notes minimized the need for adult intervention. In each case, the students' participation carried a dual benefit. It not only eased the work of the classroom's intervention but also enhanced the students' autonomy and self-determination.

A CLASSROOM ILLUSTRATION

Mrs. J, a third-grade teacher, wondered if the point system she was using to monitor students' work and behavior was detracting from the quality of her relationships with the students. In addition, the multiple demands to manage the classroom behavior were exhausting her and left her discouraged with teaching. Anonymous student surveys showed that the students were also dissatisfied with their relationship with the teacher.

Figure 7.8 shows the students' apparent alienation. Only three students said they enjoyed being a part of the class, and only three felt understood by their teacher. Mrs. J was disappointed but not surprised by the results. With her students, she cocrafted a plan to make the classroom more caring. The students enjoyed the classroom meeting held about the data and asked that this be made a regular activity of the classroom. Students also said that the pace of the classroom was quite hurried and that they had little time to share matters of personal importance. In response, Mrs. J created a "personal moment

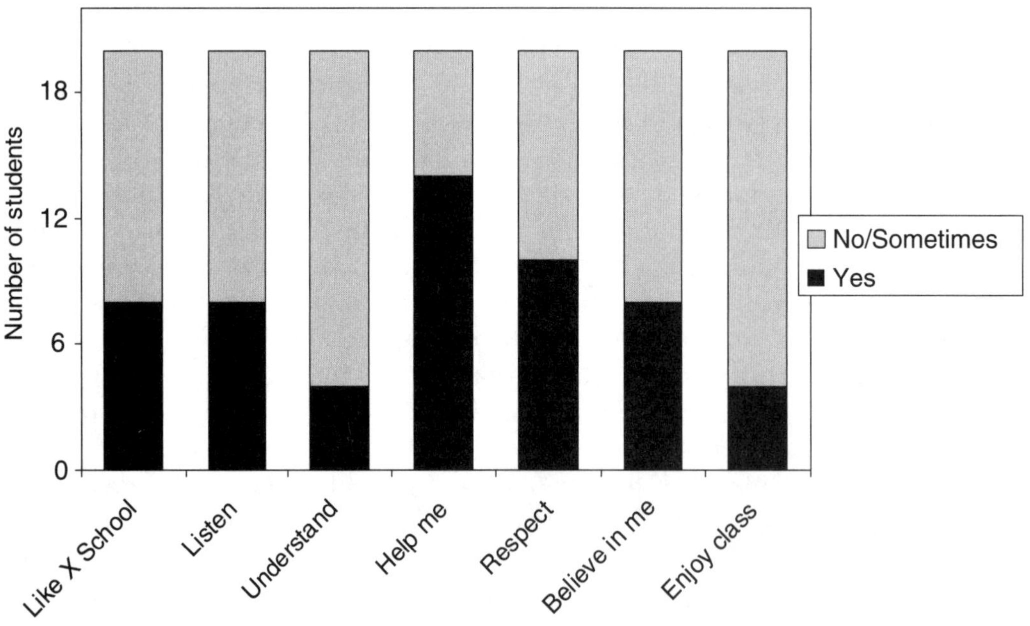

FIGURE 7.8. Example of a classroom's preintervention ClassMaps survey results for teacher–student relationships.

board" where students could sign up for a brief 5-minute "check-in" with her. The class also decided to build "getting-to-know-you" activities into some of their classroom meetings so that they could learn more about one another. (Many of these activities are described in Chapter 8.) Mrs. J made deliberate efforts to enjoy herself more while teaching: she smiled more, used more humor, and incorporated games and play into her instructional activities. She made more time for personal conversations with students, and attended some of their activities and performances outside of classroom hours. When the student surveys were recollected 5 months later, there were striking improvements in the classroom's teacher–student relationships. Figure 7.9 shows that more than 80% of the students now enjoyed the class and felt that Mrs. J understood them. While the students benefited from the changes in the classroom, Mrs. J profited the most. Her on-the-job satisfaction with teaching had improved.

SUMMARY

Until now, this book has emphasized the essential role that students play as members of the classroom ecological system. This chapter has emphasized the contributions that students can make toward understanding the classrooms' needs, identifying key strategies for change, and implementing classroom interventions. It is not clear where the

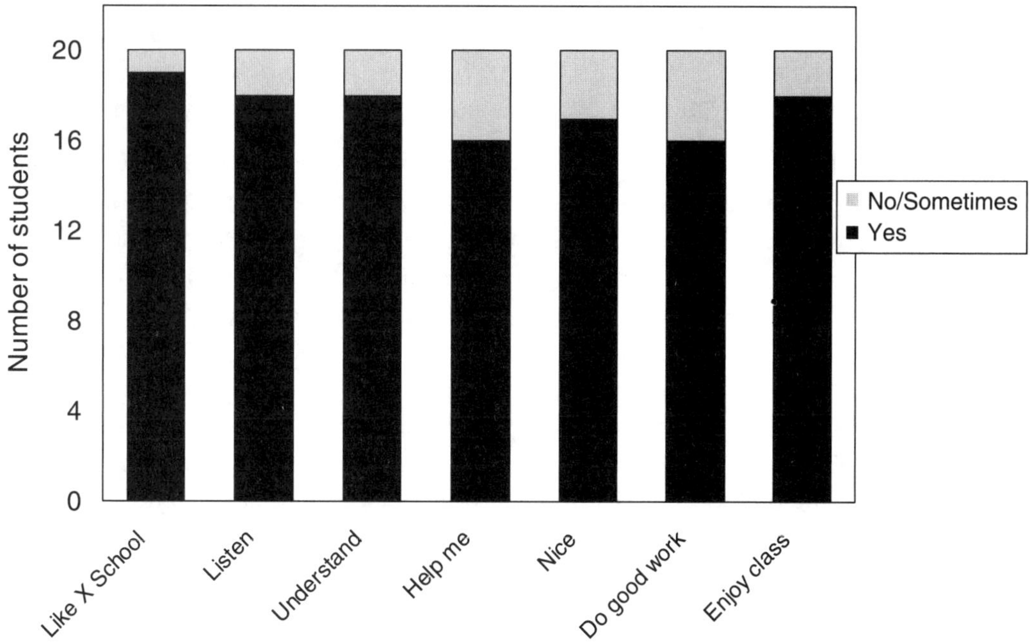

FIGURE 7.9. Example of a classroom's postintervention ClassMaps survey results for teacher–student relationships.

upper limits of student contributions lie, and it is important that their potential not be underestimated. Students are a great untapped resource of classrooms, and their contributions to classroom change can make many more things possible.

ANNOTATED BIBLIOGRAPHY

Developmental Studies Center. (1996). *Ways we want our class to be: Class meetings that build commitment to kindness and learning.* Oakland, CA: Author.

The goals and values of the Child Development Project are well represented in this brief, valuable work that describes methods for fostering a caring, productive classroom community for learning. The book reviews the essentials of classroom meetings and provides tips for dealing with many concerns that students face in typical elementary classrooms (e.g., cliques and friendship issues, appropriate behavior with substitute teachers). Using vignettes from actual classroom meetings, the book illustrates getting-to-know-you activities that facilitate a sense of trust and involvement; how to develop and implement ground rules; strategies for achieving consensus among students; methods of group facilitation, and ways to encourage and manage participation from all class members; using student suggestions for classroom change; and evaluating the effectiveness of classroom meetings.

Elias, M. J., Zins, J., Weissberg, R., Frey, K., Greenberg, M., Haynes, N., Kessler, R. Schwab-Stone, M., & Shriver, T. (1997). *Promoting social and emotional learning.* Alexandria, VA: Association for Supervision and Curriculum Development.

This valuable resource from the Association for Supervision and Curriculum Development provides an overview of social and emotional learning principles and strategies for promoting positive social–emotional and academic outcomes. Following a review of the program's philosophical underpinnings, the authors provide strategies for implementation of the program's numerous components. Educators will find strategies for supporting student's emotional intelligence and problem-solving skills, methods for involving students in community service activities, and strategies for promoting a responsive classroom community that is respectful of differences and inclusive of all students. Troubleshooting tips for overcoming systemic or financial roadblocks to implementation are provided, as well as methods for evaluating the impact of social and emotional learning programs.

Karns, M. (1994). *How to create positive relationships with students: A handbook of group activities and teaching strategies.* Champaign, IL: Research Press.

Teachers and school mental health professionals will find much to like in this easy-reading book. Karns reviews the basics of effective communication and problem-solving with students. Valuable tips and guidelines for making authentic connections with students are provided along with strategies for handling sensitive information that inevitably emerges in the classroom setting. Numerous small-group and classroom activities are described that are applicable for grades K–12. The activities are easy to implement and include strategies for group processing and debriefing. Karns's handbook is a practical one-stop shop for activities that can promote group cohesion, communication skills, and effective problem-solving strategies.

8

Developing and Implementing Effective Strategies for Classroom Change

The student and teacher comments, interpretations, and suggestions that emerged during Chapter 7's classroom meetings are the raw materials from which a plan for change will be crafted. Sometimes the classroom's students and teachers craft and implement a unique intervention strategy they have designed "from the ground up." On other occasions, the classroom team might select an informal strategy or empirically supported intervention program from the professional literature. It is important that, in addition to the classroom team, all adults and children who share the classroom participate in these decisions to select an intervention. Interventions will be implemented more completely and will be maintained longer when those affected by the intervention have a voice in its selection. The plan for intervention frequently needs to be tailored to the unique concerns of an individual classroom. Again, all key classroom participants should be included in planning for these modifications. In particular, the more involved students are in crafting, selecting, and modifying an intervention, the more likely they are to adhere to the classroom's plan.

Consider a recent example from a seventh-grade classroom. Figure 8.1 shows the data about peer relationships that were presented to students in a classroom meeting. Table 8.1 is an abbreviated transcript of the students' discussion of the data. Toward the end of the classroom discussion, students began generating some strategies that would help them feel more empowered in the class and, at the same time, more accepting of one another.

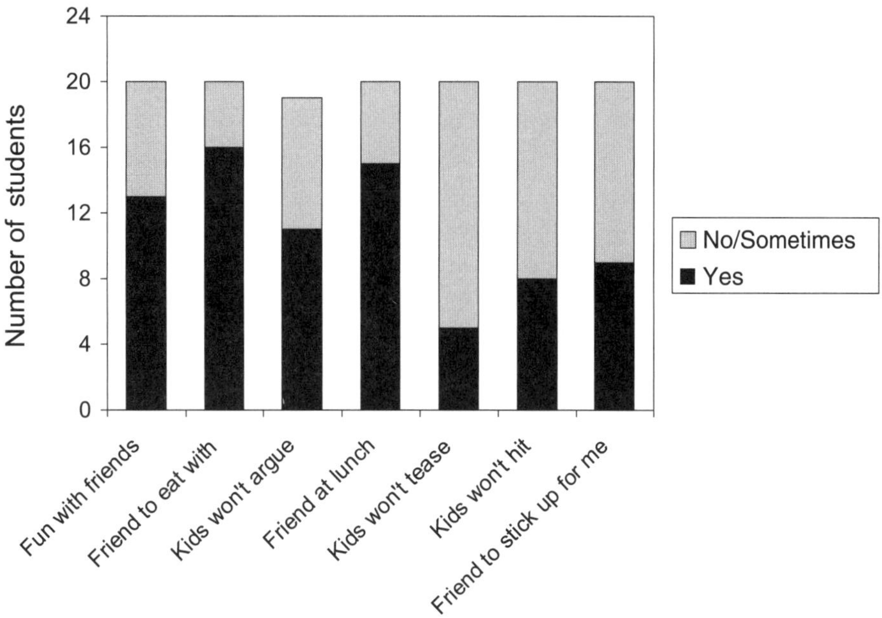

FIGURE 8.1. Example of a classroom's ClassMaps survey results for peer relationships.

INTERVENTIONS FOR THE SIX CHARACTERISTICS OF RESILIENT CLASSROOMS

Potential interventions to strengthen the resilience of classrooms are everywhere. In addition to professional journals and texts, activities to strengthen classrooms' ecological context can be found in Internet sites, newsletters and monographs, conference presentations, government publications, and research reports. There are so many recommendations for intervention that it can be difficult to isolate those that are most suitable for a target classroom. In particular, interventions should be selected with an eye toward their empirical support. An intervention is more likely to have an important impact on the classroom when there is objective research data showing that a strategy or program has worked in similar classrooms.

Interventions should also be selected because they suit the specific attributes of a target classroom. Key attributes that can alter the impact of an intervention include the demographics of the community, the resource personnel available to the classroom, and the philosophical orientation and skill of the teacher. Because of these different attributes, an antibullying program that proved highly successful in Des Moines, Iowa, might not be appropriate for a classroom in Los Angeles, California. Even comprehensive, empirically supported programs might not be suitable for a particular classroom without being extended or adapted to that classroom's unique needs. When modifying interventions, practitioners must consider the degree to which the content or format of

TABLE 8.1. Class Discussion of Sociometric Data

Q. What do you notice about this graph? Is it accurate?

A. Yes. It's accurate. Lots of kids in this class have friends to spend time with but lots of kids are saying there is hitting in the class—maybe they're the ones who are being pushed around by other kids.

Q. What do you think about that?

A. It's not OK because that makes this class not a good place. . . . It's not OK because usually if you are getting hit, even if the kid is playing around, you'll end up hitting back. There's definitely a lot of arguing that goes on all day and in other classes too.

Q. Why do you think there's so much arguing?

A. Because we are all different. People tease other kids because they're different. Sometimes it can just be fun. Yeah, but sometimes when kids finished their work they bother kids who are still working. Some kids don't even do their work. They bother lots of kids!

Q. How come that happens?

A. It's easy to lose attention if work is not at your level. Then you start bugging kids. The people who are ahead on their work should walk around and help keep an eye on things and help other kids.

Q. Raise your hands if you'd like there to be less arguing in this class.

A. (*Most of the students raised their hands.*)

Q. How could that happen?

A. We should learn how to accept other people more. It has to be individual, you have to want to not hit other kids and stop arguing. We just need to learn to respect rules before we'll ever really follow them.

Q. What would make kids respect rules more?

A. They're not our rules—we didn't make them.

Q. What if you did?

A. It would be easier to follow them. We never get to make the rules, we're just kids.

Q. Are you saying that if we let kids help make the class rules, and if we were sure to give work that was at kids level, and if we can help kids figure out ways to accept other kids who are different, then there'd be less arguing, teasing, and hitting?

A. (*Most kids agreed.*)

Q. What should we work on first?

A. We can make some different rules in the class.

Q. What kind of different rules?

A. The kids who finish their work should help other kids. . . . I mean really help, not make fun of them. Then the teacher could give good reports for kids to take home. We should also have a rule about accepting other kids. If the class was more fun and interesting, we wouldn't bother each other so much. Everyone should eat breakfast! And shut off the air conditioner. . . . It's too noisy!

the program can still yield positive results despite the alterations. In some cases, it may be more appropriate to select a different intervention strategy than to lose the integrity of the empirically supported program.

What follows is a sampling of interventions that can be used to enhance the resilience of classrooms, ranging along a continuum from programs with substantial empirical support to more informal interventions, strategies, and resources that have received positive support from practitioners in the field. Even though each intervention is listed under one of the six characteristics, many have the potential to affect several characteristics simultaneously. This is because, as explained in Chapters 3 and 4, these characteristics are strongly linked and effectiveness in one area is often related to or caused by effectiveness in another.

In all cases, evaluation of the success of these interventions needs to be embedded into the intervention plan. Even intervention programs that have strong empirical support may not show the same results in the unique setting of a specific classroom. Evaluation will be even more important for informal intervention strategies that typically have little empirical data supporting their use. The purpose of these embedded evaluations is to verify whether the resilient classroom characteristics have been adequately enhanced or whether alternative interventions are necessary. Chapters 5 and 9 provide guidance on planning and conducting these evaluations.

Teacher–Student Relationships

Pianta and Hamre's (2001) Students, Teachers and Relationship Support (STARS) Program describes a systematic, data-tested procedure for consulting with teachers in order to enhance their relationships with their students. The STARS "banking time" intervention is similar to Barkley's (1997) parent consultation program in which parents are directed to spend a prescribed amount of time with their child, each day, regardless of the child's behavior or misbehavior. The parent assumes a very different role than usual, acting more like a "sportscaster" who narrates, observes, and labels the child's play in a nondirective fashion. In the banking time intervention, the teacher spends between 5 and 15 minutes daily with a target student doing some activity of the student's choice. This positive time creates a reserve of emotional good will that allows the teacher–student relationship to withstand later conflict without deteriorating (Pianta & Hamre, 2001). While banking time is designed to be a dyadic intervention, it might be modified for classwide implementation. Mrs. J's personal moment board, described in Chapter 7, can be considered a variant of banking time that is available to all students in the classroom. In that intervention, each student selected a time to be "heard" and receive some private attention. Likewise, classroom meetings might serve this important function while impacting a whole classroom daily or weekly.

Informal interventions to support teacher–student relationships can be found in several additional resources. The Developmental Studies Center's (1996) *Ways We Want Our Class to Be* explains how to use classroom meetings to plan for back-to-school nights, prepare for substitute teachers, review classroom learning, or solve classroom relationship problems. Faber and Mazlish (1995) describe an active-listening approach to conversations between teachers and their students. Classroom teams might draw upon this reference to plan new ways of interacting that would foster more comfortable teacher–student conversations. Pianta's (1999) text on teachers' relationships with their students provides a wealth of alternative strategies that have been used to strengthen the caring and connectedness of these relationships and to minimize student dependency.

Peer Relationships

There are a number of empirically supported interventions that can foster positive peer relationships and student's social competence. The Bullying Prevention Program (Olweus, Limber, & Mihalic, 1999) alerts teachers, students, and parents to the varying and subtle forms of bullying and prepares them to respond promptly and decisively to discourage such behavior. Greenberg, Kusche, and Mihalic's (1998) Promoting Alternative Thinking Strategies (PATHS) Program teaches children emotional literacy, self-control, social competence, and interpersonal problem-solving skills. These interventions have been identified as Blueprint Model Programs by the Center for the Study and Prevention of Violence. In their book *Promoting Social and Emotional Learning,* Elias et al. (1997) describe a wide range of school-based interventions designed to promote student's social and academic competence and the quality of peer and adult interpersonal relationships. When integrated into the school curriculum, social and emotional learning (SEL) strategies have demonstrated success in promoting students' attachment to school, receptivity to learning, and academic success (Blum, McNeely, & Rinehart, 2002; Osterman, 2000). In a meta-analysis of 165 studies, Wilson, Gottfredson, and Najaka (2001) found that schools which used social and emotional learning methods extensively had improved outcomes for dropout prevention and school attendance. There are also many informal resources available for promoting school safety and violence prevention (Committee for Children, 1992; Garrity, Jens, Porter, Sager, & Short-Camilli, 2000; Ross, 1996; Sharp & Smith, 1994), strategies for social skills training in schools (Goldstein, 1999; McGinnis & Goldstein, 2000; Gresham, 2002), and programs for promoting social competence in schools (Elias & Tobias, 1996; McNamara, 2002)—all of which have potential for fostering effective peer relationships.

Social skills training programs are used frequently by school mental health professionals to address a wide range of social, behavioral, and academic concerns, including the quality of peer relationships. While there is some evidence to suggest that children with peer problems and poor social skills can benefit from such training (Bullis, Walker, & Sprague, 2001), quite recent reviews of meta-analytic studies suggest that social skills training programs typically fail to show large effects or treatment gains (Luellen, 2003). Gresham, Sugai, and Horner's (2001) review of the literature for social skills training revealed generally weak effect sizes, suggesting only very modest gain for students receiving social skills intervention. Disappointing results were also reported in meta-analyses by Quinn, Kavale, Mathur, Rutherford, and Forness (1999) and Mathur, Kavale, Quinn, Forness, and Rutherford (1998). Resilient classroom interventions have the potential to overcome critical flaws of social skills training programs in regard to generalization and maintenance of treatment effects. The most effective way to ensure the generalization and maintenance of social and academic gains is through ongoing support and modification of classroom interventions designed to strengthen those skills. Documentation of treatment adherence and treatment integrity through direct observation and frequent anonymous student surveys is an integral component of resilient classrooms.

Classroom meetings have great potential for altering the social–emotional climate in classrooms while fostering prosocial peer relationships among students (Developmental Studies Center, 1996; P. S. Murphy, 2002). Classroom meetings provide a fertile environment for the introduction of bibliotherapy strategies that can effectively address targeted classroom concerns. Doll and Doll (1997) provide a practical overview of children's mental health needs and the bibliotherapy tools and methods that can assist school personnel in meeting children's ongoing developmental needs through personalized literature. Children's books have been used to assist classrooms when students are dealing with friendship issues, bullying, and issues of loss and bereavement. One can find resources appropriate for a wide range of school-related issues across the preschool-to-high-school continuum.

Collaborative and cooperative learning activities (Wentzel & Watkins, 2002) can enhance student's engagement, achievement, and positive social communication and negotiation skills (see the last section of this chapter). Mystery Motivators (Jensen, Rhode, & Reavis, 1994) can be used to foster peer negotiations and cooperation as students work together as a whole class to earn a "mystery" reward for work completion or prosocial interactions throughout the day. Human Bingo sessions can provide the foundation for a classroom discussion of student similarities and differences. Teaching students a variety of enjoyable cooperative games can promote interpersonal cooperation, include all students in activities, and provide a suitable replacement for the more competitive playground games. Student-initiated solutions to conflict situations in the classroom can often have a beneficial impact upon student's prosocial orientation (e.g., the Welcome Wagon intervention described in Chapter 5). Engaging students in selecting and conducting whole-class service activities that support school, community, or national concerns can yield impressive results on student's self-esteem, cooperation, and social competence (Elias, 2003; Henderson & Milstein, 1996). Although many of these informal strategies have not been empirically validated, they have received high marks from practitioners for their intuitive appeal and ease of implementation. Additionally, many of these approaches can be easily adapted to the specific needs of a targeted classroom. Several of the aforementioned techniques are described in the annotated bibliography at the end of this chapter.

Home–School Relationships

An evidence-based strategy for promoting effective home–school collaboration can be found in Sheridan's (1997) model of conjoint behavioral consultation (CBC). CBC provides specific guidelines for engaging the mutual efforts of parents, teachers, and school psychologists and has yielded positive results in solving academic and behavioral problems (Sheridan, Eagle, Cowen, & Mickelson, 2001). While the focus of CBC is typically on the problems experienced by a single student, one can adapt the process when exploring solutions to classroom-level concerns. The problem-solving, collaborative nature of CBC can provide a medium for constructive, goal-directed, solution-oriented home–school partnerships. The LIFT Program (Linking the Interests of Families and Teachers; Eddy, Reid, & Fetrow, 2000) provides parents with instruction in effective discipline through six meetings at their child's school at the same time as teachers are taught more effective classroom management strategies. LIFT has been identified as a Blueprint Promising Program by the Center for the Study and Prevention of Violence.

There are numerous informal strategies for fostering home–school collaboration and shared decision making. The family–school teams described by Epstein (1995) and Christenson and Sheridan (2001) can be employed schoolwide or adapted for the classroom. In addition to improving home–school relations, this intervention can yield beneficial effects on student's academic efficacy and self-control. Home–school surveys can be effective tools when used in a collaborative manner by parents and teachers to promote problem solving and shared decision making (Christenson & Sheridan, 2001). For example, the National Standards for Parent/Family Involvement Programs (National Parent–Teacher Association, 1997) can be used as a checklist of quality indicators to identify weaknesses and plan for change. (These standards were described in Chapter 5.)

Still, the most promising strategies for connecting classrooms and families are often crafted from scratch. For example, in Chapter 3 we described a teacher who sent a letter home to parents in English and Spanish asking for permission to videotape the teacher and their child working together on typical homework problems. Similarly, students in an urban middle school were enlisted to create an art exhibit that would represent their views on the community. This fostered a great deal of home–school conversation prior to and during the exhibit. We have worked with teachers who assign students the task of interviewing their parents about the changes they have seen in schooling since they were children. Others have assigned students to ask their parents for contributions to the "suggestions-from-home" box each week. Another excellent way to foster parent involvement and improve home–school relationships is to invite parents into the building to teach crafts to children. Parents have a wide range of talents that schools can tap into, such as cooking, gardening, carpentry, and sewing. Grandparents can be invited to take a whole class on a walking history tour—bringing the past to life by sharing with the students what their community was like when these elders were in school.

Academic Efficacy

Ridley and Walther (1995) describe numerous empirically derived strategies that teachers can use to foster student's academic efficacy, even within the constraints of typical classroom grading policies and standards-based assessment. These include (1) offering extra assistance to students, even if this means time outside of regular class hours; (2) teaching for and carefully monitoring student understanding, even if this means reducing the volume of curriculum or the pace of instruction (covering less material with the goal of uncovering deeper understanding is a solid instructional strategy that also enhances efficacy); (3) avoiding any shaming, embarrassing, or cajoling of students (the research on student motivation speaks against public or private criticism [Brophy, 1987; Covington, 1992]); (4) providing quick, accurate, and detailed feedback to students; (5) focusing on effort and personal understanding rather than normative academic and social comparisons; (6) supporting students in setting appropriate and attainable academic goals in the classroom; and (7) supporting students' work within their zone of proximal development by designing tasks that shape student learning toward the ultimate instructional goal.

Zimmerman et al. (1996) provide empirically derived strategies that foster students' self-regulatory activities and sense of academic efficacy. The components of their approach include classroom support for goal setting, self-evaluation, effective note taking, and confident test-taking strategies—all designed to support students' self-confidence, academic efficacy, and personal responsibility for learning.

Academic Self-Determination

Elias and Tobias's (1996) *Social Problem Solving: Interventions in the Schools* presents an empirically derived set of strategies that can infuse problem-solving steps into the academic curriculum and social rules of schools. The approach was developed through a program of research at the "Improving Social Awareness—Social Problem Solving" Project of Rutgers University. The authors provide materials for in-service training programs, along with practical strategies that can be embedded into a classroom's daily routines and be utilized by any school staff member. The approach is centered on a set of problem-solving and decision-making steps that are critical for success in school and in life.

The following subsection includes empirically supported and informal interventions for improving student's behavioral self-control, academic efficacy, and self-determination. To avoid redundancy they are presented only in that subsection.

Behavioral Self-Control

"Think Aloud" (Camp & Bash, 1981) is a psychoeducational training program that can enhance social and cognitive problem-solving skills and foster cognitive and behavioral self-control capacities. The program was designed for use in elementary schools, with separate manuals for use in grades 1–2, 3–4, and 5–6. The program lessons can be delivered to small groups or to entire classrooms. Lessons focus upon the enhancement and modification of cognitive mediation processes to foster effective behavioral control, goal setting, social perspective taking, and students' evaluation of classroom behavior solutions based on their consequences. Studies generally support the effectiveness of the program for improving children's problem-solving, behavioral self-control, and academic performance (Camp & Bash, 1980, 1981).

Shure's (2001) "I Can Problem Solve" program teaches children to use problem-solving steps to resolve social problems that they encounter in their daily lives. The program, which emphasizes teaching children *how* to think rather than *what* to think, can enhance children's social adjustment, promote prosocial behavior, and decrease impulsivity. Although the program was designed for use with small groups of 6–10 children, the methods can be adapted for whole-classroom use. Shure and Spivac (1980, 1982) reported improvements in classroom behavior and problem-solving skills, even some 3 or 4 years after completion of the program. "I Can Problem Solve" has been recognized as a Promising Program by the Center for the Study and Prevention of Violence and by the Expert Panel on Safe, Disciplined and Drug-Free Schools (U.S. Department of Education, 2002).

Kendall and Bartel's (1990) *Teaching Problem Solving to Students with Learning and Behavior Problems* shows how teachers can incorporate problem-solving training into classroom routines. Kendall and Braswell's (1985) program "Stop & Think" teaches individual children to pause and evaluate their behavior before acting. Their research has shown this to be an effective strategy for impulsive children. Eddy and colleague's (2000) LIFT Program, described above, incorporates a Good Behavior game at recess and promotes home–school application of effective management methods.

The Technical Assistance Center on Positive Behavioral Interventions and Supports (PBIS), established by the Office of Special Education Programs, U.S. Department of Education, provides schools with capacity-building information and technical assistance for identifying, adapting, and sustaining effective schoolwide disciplinary practices. The program is founded upon the assumption that learning and teaching occur best in school climates that are positive, orderly, courteous, and safe. More than 500 schools in the United States across 13 states, elementary to high school, have implemented schoolwide PBIS. The program has demonstrated school- and districtwide benefits in decreasing behavior referrals, increasing academic instruction time, and improving academic achievement (Sugai & Horner, 2001).

The Tough Kid Books (e.g., *The Tough Kid Tool Box*; Jensen et al., 1994) provide practical strategies for managing classroom behavior problems with a minimum of teacher intervention. These books include strategies and reproducible handouts for supporting student motivation, self-monitoring, task persistence, behavior contracting, and many other practical classroom matters. Although many of the strategies were developed for use with individual children, the materials are easily adapted for whole-classroom use.

IMPROVING THE RESILIENT CHARACTERISTICS OF CLASSROOMS: AN ILLUSTRATION

A novel intervention that targeted several characteristics of resilient classrooms began with the administration of a sociogram. Students nominated three peers each for items describing a wide range of social and academic behaviors (e.g., "The kids who have a lot of friends are________________________"; "The kids who finish their work are________________________"). Figure 8.2 shows a portion of the sociogram results, tallied to represent the number of nominations a particular student received for each of the sociogram questions. Each number along the top represents a student in the classroom. The numbers were assigned randomly to ensure student anonymity.

During classroom meetings, the sociogram was placed on an overhead projector at the front of the classroom and one line at a time was uncovered as students speculated about the meaning of the numbers. Inferences were strongly encouraged as students attempted to discern why a particular student may have seven votes for "Who has a lot of friends?" yet only one vote for "Who do you want to work with on class projects?" Student inferences such as "Maybe they never pay attention" or "Maybe they're not very good at finishing their work" helped them see the relationship between classroom behaviors and their social or academic standing with their peers. The intervention helped students define specific academic and social goals they want to achieve and determined the teacher, classroom, and/or parental supports they needed to achieve those goals. In response to these discussions, students began to develop classroom-based strategies to acquire the prosocial attributes and good academic habits of a "student number" on the sociogram that they wanted to emulate. They also received considerable feedback and support from other students and the teacher. Some students chose to tape their two most important goals on their desks. The students decided to reinforce each other's progress through the use of yellow sticky-notes that would quietly reinforce the efforts of their classmates. To help keep one classmate from continually talking to his neighbors, nearby students adopted a "zipping the lips" pantomime,

Student numbers	1	2	3	4	5	6	7	8	9	10
Sociogram questions										
Who has lots of friends?	3	7	0	2	2	3	11	2	5	1
Who do you want to work with on class projects?	9	1	1	1	3	3	9	1	2	0
Who do you like to play with?	5	4	0	2	4	1	4	3	4	2
Who is liked by everyone?	3	5	0	2	2	2	8	2	4	0
Who gets good grades?	10	2	0	3	1	5	10	1	1	1
Who does not pay attention?	1	6	2	0	4	1	0	8	3	5

FIGURE 8.2. Example of a classroom's peer sociometric rating results.

coupled with a good-natured smile, to help their classmate stay focused. Teacher participation was crucial to reinforce the language and strategies of effective goal setting and prosocial behaviors on a daily level in the classroom. Through ongoing classroom meetings the adult facilitators fostered a social context for learning that supported academic goal setting, supportive relations among students and teachers, and the development of effective behavior regulation skills.

SUMMARY

This chapter described the various resources and principles that guide classroom teams in selecting effective classroom interventions. The limited availability of evidence-based interventions for classroom change often requires that teams rely on innovative but untested practices. Still, even once research on classroom intervention has matured, teams will need to continue to make clinical judgments about the suitability of any particular intervention for a specific classroom. Classrooms vary widely in their human and material resources, the nature and extent of their needs, and the unique combination of intervention activities that will shift their ecological systems. Interventions' effectiveness will vary in interaction with these unique classroom conditions. Consequently, appropriate selection of classroom interventions will always need to be preceded by a functional analysis of classroom weaknesses (Chapter 6) to identify the classroom conditions that might constrain or potentiate an intervention. Even when evidence-based interventions are available, these will always need to be monitored through the ongoing collection of classroom data (Chapter 5) to verify that the intervention is effective in each specific classroom. Responsible classroom intervention is conducted within the broader context of classroom consultation.

ANNOTATED BIBLIOGRAPHY

Elias, M. J., & Tobias, S. E. (1996). *Social problem solving: Interventions in the schools.* New York: Guilford Press.

This book presents practical, field-tested approaches to promoting critical thinking and social problem skills for students in grades K–8. The interventions have been utilized in general and special education settings and have proven successful with typically developing and high-risk students alike. The approach can be utilized in classrooms or small groups and targets such skills as behavioral self-control, group participation and social awareness, effective communication, and academic and social problem solving. Staff development tips and strategies are provided, along with practical methods for assessing progress and adapting strategies for special need students.

Gass, M. A. (1995). *Book of metaphors.* Dubuque, IA: Kendall/Hunt.
Rohnke, K. (1989). *Cowstails and cobras II: A guide to games, initiatives, ropes courses, and adventure curriculum.* Dubuque, IA: Kendall/Hunt.
Rohnke, K., & Butler, S. (1997). *Quicksilver: Adventure games, initiative problems, trust activities and a guide to effective leadership.* Dubuque, IA: Kendall/Hunt.

In these three publications, the practitioner will find a wide range of experiential activities that are appropriate for children and adolescents—in the classroom, on the playground or soccer field, or during overnight field trips. The authors are skilled, insightful experiential group leaders who provide the reader with a range of approaches to maximize the meaning of activity-based learning for group members. Gass's *Book of Metaphors* will help practitioners support students in their ability to draw metaphors between their experience in group activities (their behavior, thoughts, and feelings) and their experiences in real-life settings like the playground or the classroom. Rohnke's *Cowstails and Cobras II* provides a range of outdoor adventure-type activities (including those requiring rope course equipment) that are chosen specifically for elementary, middle, or high school students. As part counselor, teacher, or physical education specialist, the facilitator of adventure activities will wear different hats at different times—depending upon the age, cognitive level, and self-awareness of the group members. Rohnke and Butler's *Quicksilver* offers a wide range of (mostly) outdoor activities that can promote self-awareness, problem solving, and prosocial skills.

Gibbs, J. (1995). *Tribes: A new way of learning and being together.* Sausalito, CA: Center Source Systems.

Many schools, especially middle/junior high schools, are realizing that students of all ability levels feel more connected to each other, to their teachers, and to learning if their large, impersonal school and classroom environments are replaced with small, inclusive learning communities. This book is a guide for forming such inclusive, competency-supporting learning communities ("tribes") of students from preschool through high school. In heterogeneous groups of three (preschool) to five or six (high school) that remain together for an entire school year, students learn communication skills and offer each other additional "air time" when teachers may be too busy to answer questions or listen. They also learn skills for collaboration, problem solving and decision making, conflict resolution, and goal setting. The book contains detailed directions for deciding if a classroom is ready to form such tribes, securing administrative support, writing content lesson plans in a tribes process format, and pages of teaching and team-building strategies. This is an excellent book for teachers who want to reenergize or restructure their classrooms at any point in the school year.

Luckner, J. L., & Nadler R. S. (1997). *Processing the experience: Strategies to enhance and generalize learning.* Dubuque, IA: Kendall/Hunt.

This book will serve as a welcome guide for those who are new to classroom interventions and/or experiential group work. Based on substantive research from such fields as psychotherapy, neuroscience, spirituality, and education, this book illuminates the rationale for experientially based education and offers an elegant "how-to" guide for processing group experiences in a wide range of psychoeducational settings. The authors give you everything you need to know to help group/classroom participants internalize new information and awareness in a way that is meaningful and coherent. In contrast to remembering one's experiences, it is the processing of the experience that leads to understanding and integration. Like constructivist teachers, effective group leaders foster linkages between psychoeducational activities and one's own life experience to maximize learning. This book is a must-have for anyone working with children and adolescents in groups or classrooms.

Ridley, D. S., & Walther, B. (1995). *Creating responsible learners: The role of a positive classroom environment.* Washington, DC: American Psychological Association.

This monograph is part of the Psychology in the Classroom series produced through collaborative efforts of APA Division 15 (Educational Psychology) and APA Books. It provides useful research-based strategies for crafting classroom environments that foster student's motivation, responsibility, and self-directed learning efforts. In a clear, practical manner, the book describes strategies for promoting students' social and academic self-efficacy, sense of belonging within the classroom environment, and participation in crafting meaningful learning experiences. A framework for implementing a student-directed approach to classroom discipline is provided along with evaluation strategies and tips for overcoming obstacles to implementation.

Witt, J., LaFleur, L., Naquin, G., & Gilbertson, D. (1999). *Teaching effective classroom routines.* Longmont, CO: Sopris West.

This is an extraordinarily useful guidebook that walks teachers through systematic strategies for teaching students daily routines that make teaching easier. Common routines include following directions, sharpening pencils, paying attention on command, following directions, or passing out and passing in papers. Each step in the routine is described, and instructions describe how to introduce and manage the routine and how to use a camera-ready overhead transparency to support the classroom lesson. These units are especially useful for classrooms with high levels of disruptive behaviors or for classrooms with beginning teachers who are still learning classroom management skills.

Zimmerman, B. J., Bonner, S., & Kovach, R. (1996). *Developing self-regulated learners: Beyond achievement to self-efficacy.* Washington, DC: American Psychological Association.

Another monograph in the APA Psychology in the Classroom series, *Developing Self-Regulated Learners* offers an integrated approach to promoting student self-regulation, goal setting, and behavioral self-control. Following a brief synopsis of the pertinent literature, the authors provide an integrated set of strategies that teacher can use to "work themselves out of the job of managing their students' learning." Methods for promoting students' planning and time management skills, comprehension, summarization and writing skills, and test anticipation and preparation techniques are described in a clear and practical manner. The teacher's role in supporting student goal setting, self-evaluation and monitoring of progress is brought to life through realistic classroom examples and practical reproducible tables, charts, and monitoring forms.

COOPERATIVE GAMES USED SUCCESSFULLY IN THIRD THROUGH SIXTH GRADES

Rock–Paper–Scissors Tag

Rock–Paper–Scissors Tag is a game that students can quickly learn to play independently (Fluegelman, 1976).

Materials

A large playing area.

Description

Students are split into two "teams" and each goes to one side of the gym or playing field. Members of each team then huddle to decide if they are going to be rock, paper, or scissors. The two teams then meet in the middle and call out to each other "1, 2, 3." On "3," each team shows its chosen sign. The team that "wins" then chases the other team to their end of the playing field. If a participant is caught prior to reaching his or her team's base (the wall of the gym or some other predetermined marker), that student must go over to the other team. After the activity, students commented on how they often switched teams, so that whose team you started on (often a point of contention in competitive games) was not important. They also pointed out that the game ended only if time ran out, thus leaving everyone a winner.

The Hula-Hoop Circle

The Hula-Hoop Circle highlights the importance of teamwork (Rohnke & Butler, 1997).

Materials

One Hula-Hoop.

Description

The entire group forms a circle holding hands. A Hula-Hoop is placed between two players. The group's goal is to move the Hula-Hoop around the circle without letting go of one another. As the group begins to master the idea, we start timing them to see how fast they can get the Hula-Hoop around the circle. This activity can be used frequently to remind students of the importance of teamwork. Following the activity, students discussed the importance of team cooperation, the different strategies that individuals used, and how one person's best strategy was not always someone else's best strategy, making it important to allow others to use the ideas that work best for them.

Hog-Call

Hog-Call is a game that fosters group cooperation (Gass, 1995).

Materials

Cloth that can be used for blindfolds.

Description

First describe the game to students. Then divide them into pairs. Each student pair is to pick a compound word or two words that go together (e.g., high–school, peanut–butter, salt–pepper). Each student in a pair is assigned one part of the compound word. One student in each pair goes to one end of the gym or field and his or her partner goes to the other end. After being blindfolded, the students hold their hands out in front of them in *the safety position,* with their palms facing the other group. When the facilitator shouts "Go," the students must find their partner by walking slowly and calling out the word assigned to them. The game was followed by an interesting discussion about finding enjoyment when working with other students who one might not know very well and how every student had an opportunity to choose the word(s) to *hog-call.*

Human Bingo

Human Bingo is a fun activity that fosters familiarity and group cohesion (Feigelson, 1998). It can be played before a classroom meeting or problem-solving group discussion, or when there is a need for movement and conversation in the classroom.

Materials

Human Bingo forms, clipboards (Figure 8.3).

Human Bingo

B	I	N	G	O
Has traveled outside the country ______	Has more than 3 TV sets in their house ______	Plays on a sports team ______	Is an only child ______	Whole family lives together ______
Favorite food is pizza ______	Has been snow-shoeing ______	Has been to the Grand Canyon ______	Has ridden a horse ______	Was born in another state ______
Has two families ______	Has been to a Colorado Rockies game ______	☆ Has a teacher from Scotland ______	Plays a musical instrument ______	Gets an allowance ______
Is left-handed ______	Has a collection of something ______	Has more than two pets ______	Has eaten sushi ______	Favorite subject is math ______
Has been camping ______	Has a dog ______	Has a big brother ______	Has been to an ocean ______	Has more than 5 people living with him or her ______

FIGURE 8.3. Example of a Human Bingo card.

Description

Each student is given a Human Bingo sheet and a clipboard. The students are allowed to walk around the room, finding peers who have certain characteristics such as "more than one pet" or "no brothers or sisters."

Once a template is designed in a word processor, the content of the Human Bingo squares can be changed frequently according to student's interests or to generate familiarity. The game can serve as a springboard for class discussion on selected topics (e.g., "Who lives with a step-parent?" or "Who has had to stay overnight in the hospital?"). When students find someone with the defined characteristic, they ask that person to sign his or her name in the appropriate square. When a student gets bingo, he or she can choose a whole-class reward or some predetermined activity that the whole class enjoys.

9

Evaluating the Impact on Students

National policymakers suggest that the route to improving schools and classrooms is very simple (No Child Left Behind Act of 2001; H.R. 1, 107th Congress, 2001). Schools simply need to find out "what works" and do it. There is good truth in this logic. Educators should provide solid empirical evidence that the services they provide are effective in improving the academic and personal success of their students. Still, the "what works" argument assumes that it is a straightforward task for researchers to identify effective programs and for schools to restrict their practices to only those programs. Unfortunately, finding out what works is far more difficult than it seems. National leaders are still debating the criteria that must be met in order for an intervention to be declared effective (Chambless & Hollon, 1998; Lonigan, Elbert, & Bennett-Johnson, 1998; Weisz, 1998), and the task of identifying effective classwide interventions is even more daunting (Doll et al., 2000). In the meantime, while the national debates proceed, educators will often need to document the impact of their services on a case-by-case basis. This chapter explains how to conduct evaluations that can demonstrate whether resilient classroom interventions have "worked."

Until this point, this book has described data collection as an integral part of classroom intervention, with the purpose of identifying when a classroom's goal for change has been met. It is tempting to equate the evaluation of resilient classroom programs with a simple measurement task. If a classroom's peer relationships were shown to be contentious initially, and if classmates were interacting frequently and comfortably after a classwide intervention, it might seem reasonable to claim that the intervention was effective. However, the classroom could have changed for reasons that are completely independent of the planned intervention. For example, the frequency of recess conflicts dropped dramatically once an assistant principal replaced the missing tetherballs, moved the four-square court to a better location, and had goals and sidelines painted onto the soccer fields; or when a school librarian began to allow some students to spend recess in the computer lab instead of going outside; or when a school's physical education teachers introduced a revised curriculum that taught children a number of games that they could play at recess. School changes like these could have been the cause of a classroom's improved peer relationships instead of the teacher's intervention.

Not every resilient classroom intervention needs a comprehensive and rigorous evaluation. When a teacher and a classroom team are working together to enhance a classroom's characteristics, they simply need to know that the conditions for learning have improved. If student conflicts drop or teacher–student relationships improve, it is relatively unimportant to know who should receive credit for the improvement. However, in some situations a school's allocation of resources or a classroom's access to funding may be influenced by evidence that a classroom intervention program is empirically effective.

Convincing program evaluations not only demonstrate whether conditions in classrooms improve once an intervention is used but also examine whether the changes were due to the intervention and assess the size of the impact on student success. A well-conducted evaluation begins with a clear decision about the purpose of the intervention program: What will be changed and how much must it change in order for the program to be considered a success. (Chapters 2, 3, and 4 of this book discuss the intervention goals that are likely to make classrooms more resilient communities for children.) Next, a measurement strategy must be identified that allows for the collection of data that are objective and quantifiable. (Chapter 5 describes several alternative assessment tools to assess classroom characteristics.) Then, baseline data must be gathered to determine the preintervention characteristics of classrooms. The intervention must be described as a very specific, step-by-step plan, and careful records must be kept to document whether it is implemented exactly according to the plan in all classrooms participating in the intervention. There must be an evaluation design that specifies a schedule for collecting data and implementing the intervention so that it is possible know whether classroom improvements are due to the intervention. Finally, the evaluation data must be reviewed and used to decide whether and how to refine the intervention to improve its effectiveness.

CLARIFYING THE PURPOSE

Resilient classroom interventions will have one of six immediate goals: to improve a classroom's teacher–student relationships, peer relationships, home–school relationships, academic efficacy, self-determination, or behavioral self-control. In some cases, one or more components of these goals will be selected instead. For example, a goal for classroom change might be to reduce the number of fights and conflicts that occur on the playground or to increase the frequency with which children talk with their parents about their schoolwork. When ClassMaps surveys were used to assess classroom characteristics, teachers frequently built their goals for change around one or more items on the surveys. Each of these goals is designed to alter the classroom's ecology so that it becomes a more successful place for children to learn and develop. Because they are immediate goals of the intervention, these are the goals that are most likely to be met. Immediate goals should always be defined for an evaluation.

Still, these immediate goals may not be highly valued by administrators, community members, government officials, or policymakers, especially if they are not convinced that resilient classroom contexts will improve students' academic success. These external audiences to the classroom are typically interested in goals that target student outcomes: higher test scores, lower grade retention rates, lower dropout rates, lower suspension or expulsion rates, and higher student grades. These are indirect goals of the intervention and, if they are somewhat removed from the immediate activities of the classroom interventions, these goals are less likely to be met over a short period of intervention. Still, the importance of these goals cannot be underestimated because they may determine whether or not resources will be available to continue an intervention, promote a teacher, or allocate staff time to a classroom or building. Student outcome goals should be established whenever important decisions about resources, access, or school policy might be made based upon results of the evaluation.

Intermediate goals lie in between immediate intervention goals and student outcome goals. An assumption of resilient classrooms is that effective classroom environments will increase children's availability for learning by increasing their academic engagement and enhancing their behavioral discipline. Consequently, goals set for improvements in academic engagement and class discipline will represent middle steps between goals set for more effective classroom environments and goals set for improved student outcomes. While external audiences might not value attainment of these intermediate goals as highly as they value better student outcomes, the relationship between more time on task and academic success is more apparent and easier to defend than is that between classroom characteristics and academic success. Moreover, changes will be noticed in these intermediate goals over shorter time intervals than those for the student outcome goals. For these reasons, it can be very useful to track progress toward these intermediate goals.

Clearly, then, defining the purpose of a classroom intervention is not as simple as it may first appear. Goals may differ depending on whether they are set by the teacher alone, with the participation of the classroom's student or families, or by an administrator or policymaker. The purpose of the evaluation can shift decidedly depending on whether the audience is the classroom only or a building-level administrator, or whether urgent decisions are being made based on the evaluation.

Time is a critical component of any intervention goal. The purpose of an intervention is never to alter a classroom "eventually" or given sufficient time. Instead, the intervention is successful if it accomplishes its goal within a reasonable time frame. It is reasonable to expect a classroom social skills curriculum to alter the social behaviors of a classroom's students within some 8–12 weeks. It is less reasonable to expect such a curriculum to alter the children's social behaviors within a few days. Consequently, well-stated goals include a statement about the time interval over which change is expected to occur. When a classroom's students are participants in the goal setting, it is important to recognize the developmental differences that exist in children's ability to track goals over time. As a rule of thumb, most middle school students can track progress toward a goal that they are expected to achieve within a month's time but find it very difficult to stay focused on goals that will be achieved a semester or a year into the future. For example, a sixth-grade teacher had a very difficult time motivating students to work toward a trip to the Mesa Verde prehistoric cliff dwellings in southwestern Colorado scheduled for 2 years later. Elementary school students can easily track progress toward goals that they expect to achieve within a week or even two, but they generally lose interest in working toward goals that are several weeks in the future. Many high school students can work toward goals that are a semester away but may not plan well toward goals that are displaced a year or more into the future.

Most evaluation designs require the replication of an intervention across more than one classroom or across more than one characteristic of a classroom. Consequently, evaluations of classroom interventions are usually directed toward high-frequency goals of classroom change: increasing homework or seatwork completion, enhancing teacher relationships, improving communication with families, or reducing peer conflict.

MEASUREMENT STRATEGIES

The selection of measures for classroom characteristics has been described in some detail in Chapter 5. These assessment strategies are usually satisfactory for gathering data about the immediate goals of resilient classroom interventions. Information about student outcome goals—suspension and expulsion rates, test scores, graduation rates, report card grades—are collected as a matter of course in most schools. The only challenge in assessing these goals is accessing the information for the specific classroom.

Assessments of intermediate goals related to academic engagement and behavioral discipline are more challenging. In most cases, indicators related to these goals are integral to the record keeping of a classroom. For example, student attendance, work completion rates, and homework completion rates ought to be recorded in classroom record books. However, in actual practice, these records may be very haphazard and lack the dependability necessary for data collection. In these cases, keeping stricter records of classroom performance may become part of the intervention plan.

A strategy for tracking the academic engagement of students with disabilities is integral to the Check and Connect Program for dropout prevention (Sinclair, Christenson, Hurley, & Evelo, 1998). The program maintained daily records of student tardies, truancies, and behavioral referrals. In addition, teachers completed weekly rating forms describing student work completion and classroom time-on-task. The Check and Connect Program intervened with students when these records showed a pattern of disengagement from school. Like many of the measures that have been described in Chapter 5, the Check and Connect record keeping is intended to focus on individual students at risk and would need modification before being used to track classroom engagement.

It is also possible to use direct observation to record academic time-on-task within a classroom. Squires and Joyner (1996) describe a simple procedure for observing academic engaged time in a classroom. A trained observer spends ten 10-minute intervals in a classroom. During each interval, the observer looks at each individual student for 2–3 seconds, decides whether that student is on task, and enters a tally mark on an observation form if the student is not engaged. The observer continues until all students in the class have been observed, then repeats the process for each of the 10-minute intervals. At the end of the observation, a simple calculation yields the engagement rate for the classroom.

Regardless of the data collection procedures that are used, an effective program evaluation requires that the data be gathered strictly, precisely, and completely. Missing or incomplete data seriously impair the ability to draw firm conclusions from the evaluation. A corollary rule is that the data must be extremely simple to collect. Complicated data collection procedures are easily violated, whereas sensible and easy-to-follow procedures are more likely to yield complete information. Only persons who have no vested interest in the evaluation results should collect evaluation data. For example, when students in a classroom participate in evaluating ClassMaps survey information and plan a classroom intervention with the teacher, it is important that the students not be the only source of evaluation data. Because of their participation, they will want to believe that things are getting better in their class and may not provide entirely objective information about class changes.

There are a number of strategies that classrooms teams can use to simplify data collection. Especially when multiple measures are being collected, more than one person should be participating in data collection. For example, we have had good success in assigning a responsible classroom student with the task of collecting an after-recess survey. It is sometimes possible to use data that are already being collected for another purpose. If existing data are not available, often it is feasible to use data that can be constructed from permanent products of the system and can be coded retrospectively. Finally, the team should construct simple forms, charts, and tables as memory and organizational aids to capture the data.

BASELINE DATA

The purpose of baseline data is to show the status of classrooms prior to any intervention. To accomplish this, sufficient baseline data must be collected to provide a convincing description of the preintervention classrooms. Generally this requires a minimum of five—preferably at least seven—data points. If these data points provide a consistent and stable picture of the classroom's characteristics, intervention activities can then begin. However, if these data points are highly inconsistent or show that the classroom's status is gradually improving or gradually worsening, a longer period of baseline data collection might be required. Ideally, the baseline data should provide a clear, uncontested prediction about the projected future status of the classroom if no intervention were to occur.

The collection of baseline data can be difficult to defend in schools. When assessment has provided clear evidence of a problem in a classroom, there can be tremendous pressure to proceed immediately into the intervention without pausing for more baseline assessment. For these reasons, the lack of baseline data is the most frequent violation of school-based program evaluations. Without baseline data, it is virtually impossible to determine whether a classroom is improving.

In some cases, existing data may provide a good baseline for an intervention. For example, when a second-grade classroom decided to plan a homework completion project, the teachers' record book had 3 months of baseline data on the rates of homework completion. Existing records may also document preintervention attendance rates, grades, test performance, or home–school communications. In some classrooms, there is an archive of completed work in student folders that might provide preintervention baseline data on work accuracy rates. Office discipline records may note when and how often students were sent to the school office because of behavioral violations. In some cases, the baseline rates might be known to be zero. For example, a teacher may know that she has never had a phone call from a parent or that students have never volunteered to create a lesson for the class.

INTERVENTION PLAN

When a team is working to alter the characteristics of a single classroom, decisions about how to intervene should be made in collaboration with the teacher and students who teach and learn there. Not only are these the participants with the most immediate understanding of what is needed in the classroom, but they are also those who will be responsible for implementing any intervention. However, when practitioners are working to demonstrate the impact of an intervention program in multiple classrooms, decisions about how to intervene must be based on what is likely to work in most classrooms. At the same time, intervention programs need to be selected with an eye toward what has been proven to be effective. While few classroom interventions have been verified as "empirically supported treatments," there are a number of promising practices in each of the six resilience characteristics. These have been described in Chapters 3, 4, and 8.

Once an intervention plan is made, it is critically important that a written manual describe what to do, when to do it, and to whom to assign the task. Like individual classroom interventions, if this plan is written in a checklist format, it can be used to keep a weekly record of the steps that were carried out and those that were inadvertently omitted. These written records will verify that the intervention was actually used as planned in all classrooms participating in the evaluation.

Good intervention plans will specify the time over which the intervention will be used. In some cases, interventions will incorporate permanent changes to classroom routines and practices. However, in other cases, an intervention will die a natural death once it is no longer necessary. There needs to be a decision about the reasonable interval for an intervention plan to be implemented, and this should become uniform across the classrooms participating in the intervention.

EVALUATION DESIGN

Standards governing the evaluation of interventions have been described at length in the literature. To be proven effective, an intervention should have been evaluated through random-assignment control group designs in which two groups of participants are randomly assigned to intervention and no-intervention groups, and the same baseline and intervention data are collected throughout the study (Lonigan et al., 1998; Chambless et al., 1996). At the end of the study, the difference between the intervention group and the control group can be used to estimate the effect of the intervention. In a resilient classroom evaluation, however, the participant in the intervention is a *classroom* and not a *student*. Outside of a funded research study, it is rarely practical to recruit sufficient classrooms to participate in a traditional control group study. Moreover, given the diversity of conditions that exist in classrooms, it is unlikely that the same intervention would be appropriate to large numbers of classrooms. Consequently, evaluations of classrooms are best conducted using single-subject research designs in which the classroom acts as its own control group (Doll et al., 2000).

Case Studies

A case study provides the weakest of the single-subject designs. In a systematic case study, baseline data are collected (condition A), then the intervention is implemented (condition B) and intervention data are collected. This is also called an A-B design. The problem with the A-B design is that there is no good evidence that changes in the classroom are different from those that would have occurred without the intervention. While the baseline data provide a prediction of the future status of the classroom, that prediction is not confirmed. Kazdin (1982) suggests that case study designs are a simple way to establish the initial promise of an intervention but should always be followed up by designs with better controls. Still, if sufficient numbers of well-controlled case studies have been conducted, they can be aggregated to provide an estimate of the impact of the intervention across multiple conditions. For example, Sheridan et al. (2001) demonstrated the impact of conjoint behavioral consultation by aggregating CBC effect sizes across 57 consultation case studies. Aggregated case studies are most convincing if the different case examples had similar goals or used similar interventions.

One variation of an A-B design provides more convincing evidence of intervention effectiveness. In an A-B design with follow-up, the progress of the classroom continues to be monitored through data collection even after an intervention has been completed and discontinued. Then, if the classroom's characteristics begin to decline, the intervention is implemented once again. If conditions improve after the intervention is reimplemented, there is good support for suggesting that the intervention was effective in creating the change.

Withdrawal Designs

In a withdrawal design, baseline data are collected (condition A), the intervention is implemented (condition B), and once intervention data are stable the intervention is withdrawn and the classroom returns to its baseline condition (condition A). Withdrawal designs are sometimes called A-B-A designs and include many variations: A-B-A-B designs are withdrawal designs that end on an intervention phase rather than a baseline phase; A-B-A-C designs are withdrawal designs that examine two interventions (conditions B and C) rather than a single one. These can be powerful designs to use when a classroom needs to know which of two interventions is the better one to use.

Withdrawal designs are powerful because the classroom serves as its own baseline. However, these designs can only be used when the intervention is something that can be taken away. For example, if an intervention involved teaching a group of students a new strategy for resolving peer conflicts, it could not be assumed that they unlearned that strategy during the withdrawal period. Consequently a withdrawal design would not be appropriate for this kind of intervention. However, if an intervention involved holding regular classroom meetings to resolve conflicts from recess, it would be simple to stop holding the meetings during the withdrawal period. A withdrawal design would be appropriate in this instance.

There are some instances in which it would be unethical to withdraw an intervention that appears to be working. For example, when a sixth-grade teacher found that his students' suspension and expulsion rates dropped once games were provided for the recess playground, he was unwilling to withhold those games for fear that physical fights and the accompanying suspensions would resume. In most instances, these ethical issues can be solved because the withdrawal period will be of short duration and will be followed by reinstatement of the intervention.

Multiple-Baseline Designs

When the same intervention will be used to change more than one characteristic of a classroom or when the same intervention will be used for the same goal in more than one classroom, a multiple-baseline design can be used. To use a multiple baseline across goals, baseline data should be collected for both intervention goals. Then, once the baseline data are stable, the intervention should be used to change one characteristic of the classroom only. Intervention data are then collected for that goal while baseline data continue to be collected for the other goal. Once the intervention data are stable, the intervention can be used to also change the second characteristic of the classroom. There is evidence that the intervention was responsible for the classroom change if the data show that the first characteristic improved when the intervention began and that the second characteristic did not improve until the second intervention began. For example, a classroom might use classroom meetings as an intervention to discuss and problem solve peer conflicts that occur during the lunchtime recess and those that occur in class during small-group time. Baseline data would be collected to count both recess conflicts and group-time conflicts. Then, the class meetings would begin to discuss recess problems while data were still collected about both recess and group-time conflicts. Once recess conflicts declined, the class meetings could begin to discuss group-time conflicts. If these also declined, there would be good evidence to claim that classroom meetings were effective in reducing peer conflicts.

Multiple baselines can be used in the same way to evaluate an intervention that occurs in more than one classroom. If three third-grade classrooms had difficulties with students' homework completion, a multiple-baseline design would collect data on homework completion in all three classrooms until the baseline data were stable. Then, a parent involvement program could be initiated in classroom 1 while data collection continued in all three classrooms. Once the intervention data were stable in classroom 1, the parent involvement program could be added in classroom 2. Similarly, once intervention data were stable in classrooms 1 and 2, the program could be added to classroom 3. If the data showed that homework completion rates improved only once the parent involvement program was added to each class, there would be good evidence that the improvements were due to the intervention program.

REVIEW AND FEEDBACK

A critical step in any program evaluation is the periodic review of the evaluation results, then planning revisions in response to those results. Where intervention programs have not been effective, revised plans might include strengthening the dosage of the intervention, implementing it more accurately, persisting at it for an additional period of time, or changing to a new intervention. Again, careful evaluation designs will require that these modifications be made uniformly across classrooms and that data be collected systematically before, during, and after modifications.

Where interventions have been effective, it is important to decide whether the classroom goals have been met to the satisfaction of participants in the classroom.

Meaningful change in classrooms should not only be empirically detectible but should also be sufficient to satisfy the classrooms' teachers, students, and parents.

To document the classroom satisfaction with the intervention, program evaluators could adapt the Behavioral Intervention Rating Scale (BIRS; Elliott & Von Brock Treuting, 1991; Von Brock & Elliott, 1987) for use by teachers and parents. The BIRS has been used with good reliability in similar school-based studies of treatment effectiveness (Sheridan & Steck, 1995). Alternatively, Goal Attainment Scales can be used to assess students' and teachers' beliefs about whether classroom goals were met (Kiresuk, Smith, & Cardillo, 1994). A Goal Attainment Scale is a simple 5-point line stretching from –2 to +2 that is drawn on a paper. Students or teachers would circle –2 if the classroom's situation had got significantly worse, they would circle +2 if the classroom goals had been completely met, or they could mark any point in between. The midpoint of the line (0) would represent the case where nothing had changed. The validity and reliability of Goal Attainment Scales has been shown to be high when they are used in similar evaluations (Kirusek et al., 1994).

PRESENTATION OF EVALUATION RESULTS

Once an evaluation has provided convincing evidence of an intervention's effectiveness, results should be disseminated in ways that influence key decision makers. Presentations are more striking if they are brief and highly focused on the most essential information about the intervention program: What was done in the intervention? What resources were required to implement it? How much impact did it have on student success? And what policies, resources, and/or decisions are necessary to continue to use the intervention in future classrooms? Bulleted lists, highlighting, and liberal use of headings and titles will draw the audience's eye to important information. The use of data graphs and diagrams will be more influential than numbers in tables. Evaluations that occur without such careful plans for dissemination will have minimal impact.

AN EVALUATION OF A CLASSROOM INTERVENTION

P. S. Murphy (2002) evaluated the impact of classroom meetings on the recess problems of fourth- and fifth-grade students. He identified three classrooms that had too many recess problems with student conflicts (identified in Figure 9.1 as "conflict") and with students being left out (identified in Figure 9.1 as "inclusion"). In all three classrooms, he immediately began collecting two recess reports each week by having students complete a seven-item survey describing problems they had that day immediately as they came in from recess. Baseline data collection continued in all three classrooms from weeks 1 through 3. During weeks 4 and 5, once his baseline data was stable, he began to hold one classroom meeting each week in class 1 only. The meetings used a problem-solving format that consisted of asking students to describe the recess problems, suggest alternative solutions, anticipate the consequences of each solution, choose one strategy, and try it out. The classroom teacher sat at the back of the class and took notes to make sure he followed the agreed-upon meeting format. Figure 9.1 shows that the number of recess problems dropped once the meetings began. In week 6, the classroom meetings were stopped in class 1 and started in class 2; at that point, recess problems rose in class 1 but did not show any apparent change in class 2. In fact, over the entire period of class 2's classroom meetings, recess problems seemed to increase. In week 7, classroom meetings were resumed in class 1 and were initiated for the first time in class 3, and recess problems dropped in both classrooms. Murphy's assessment is an example of a simple evaluation of a classroom intervention. His results suggest that the classroom meetings were responsible for slight declines in recess problems in classes 1 and 3 but were not consistently effective in all classrooms.

SUMMARY

Rigorous evaluation of resilient classroom interventions will not always be necessary. In many classrooms where the immediate task is to refine the classroom context for learning, simple case study collection of baseline and intervention data can demonstrate that this has been accomplished. When it does occur, the purpose of evaluation will almost always be to justify school or classroom resources. In this event, three key questions will need to be answered: Were the resilient classroom interventions effective in improving classroom environments? Did students experience more success as a result? And how big was the effect?

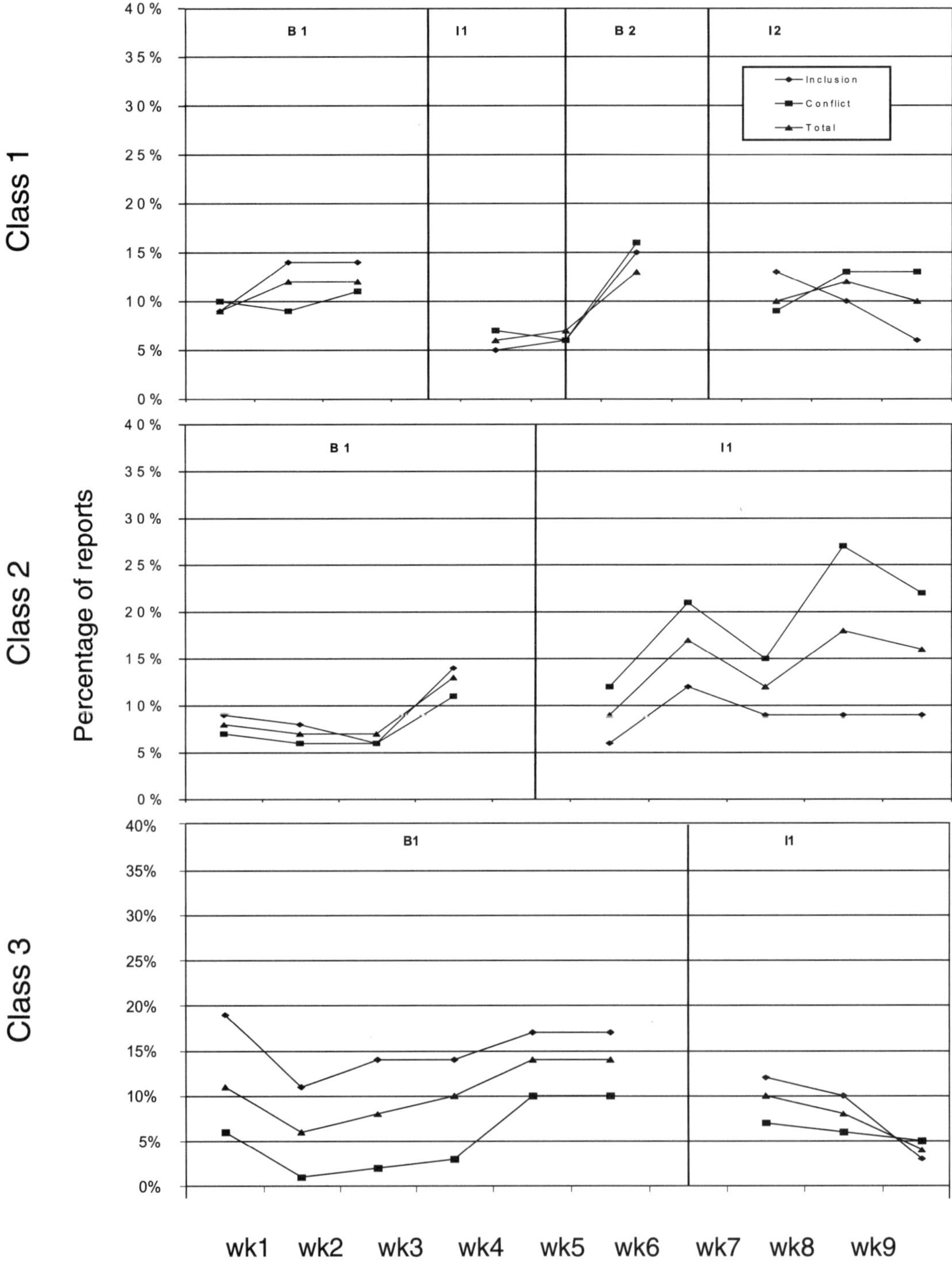

FIGURE 9.1. Trend line of students' weekly report of overall recess problems. From P. S. Murphy (2002). Reprinted by permission of the author.

10

Integrating the Resilient Classroom with Existing School Mental Health Services

Like classrooms, schools are ecological systems. Introducing change into schools requires the same careful attention as is required by changing classrooms. Large and sudden changes are difficult to sustain because they impose too many unfamiliar demands on the system. Small and subtle changes are easily co-opted; what appears at first to be a change comes to look very much like the same old practice given time. The true challenge is to integrate change into the existing practices of school while still protecting the innovative and important modifications that it represents. This chapter describes how to integrate the resilient classroom thinking into existing practices of schools. First, we describe how resilient classrooms are similar to current practices of schools, because this familiarity should ease acceptance of the change and should point to the competencies that schools already have that can support classroom interventions. Then, we review the features of resilient classrooms that are distinctive from current school practices and explain once again why these ought to be protected.

THE FAMILIAR

Much of what has been described in this book should be familiar to schools. For example, the data-based decision making that characterizes resilient classroom practices is also integral to diagnostic teaching, in which teachers systematically identify their students' strengths and weaknesses, deliver instruction that addresses the weaknesses, and reassess the results to determine whether the instruction has been successful. Data collection and analysis is also characteristic of action research, in which teachers and other practitioners systematically investigate problems of practice that they encounter in their daily work and identify optimal teaching strategies or preventive practices to address these problems. In special education programs, the progress of students is tracked through continuous collection of data so that the programs can demonstrate that the students' individual educational programs are appropriately accommodating for the disabilities. As a result of schools' growing emphasis on data-based decision making, much of the expertise that is required by resilient classroom practices already exists in schools. Most schools already have staff who understand how to collect and record data, have a foundation of knowledge about alternative ways to assess academic, social, behavioral, and emotional variables, and have a tacit understanding of ways in which data can support effective decision making.

The systematic consultation that underlies resilient classroom strategies is also familiar to schools. For the past 30 years, school mental health professionals like school psychologists, school counselors, and school social workers have been engaging in professional consultation to assist teachers with unusually difficult student problems. It has been repeatedly demonstrated that consultation is more effective when it is deliberate, highly structured, and data driven. More recently, schools have established team consultation programs in which a group of colleagues works together to assist teachers with persistent learning or behavior problems of students. These teams are variously called prereferral intervention teams (Kovaleski, 2002), instructional support teams (Kovaleski, Tucker, & Stevens, 1996), or mainstream assistance teams (Fuchs, Fuchs, & Bahr, 1990). School-based problem-solving teams have a proven record of success when permitted to provide systemic solutions to students' presenting problems (Quinn, Osher, Hoffman, & Hanley, 1998) and, when schools routinely address student learning problems within these student assistance teams prior to referring students to special education programs, 85% of students need no further evaluation for special education (Hartman & Fay, 1996). Because consultation is a familiar practice in schools, classroom teachers have become accustomed to inviting a team of colleagues to assist with classroom change and generally expect classroom consultation to be structured and rigorous.

Functional behavior assessment is an ongoing practice in most schools. It examines functional relationships between environmental variables and the occurrence or nonoccurrence of a student's behavior. Hypotheses are developed about the variables that might be causing the problem behavior, and these variables are manipulated in order to test the hypotheses. Experience with functional behavior assessment prepares schools to understand and identify the functional relationships that resilient classroom teams identify between classroom characteristics and students' success and achievement.

School have responded to public demands for excellence with buildingwide and districtwide school reforms that raise academic standards and prepare students for future employment (Dwyer, 2002). To guide reforms, many schools have a building leadership team with representatives that cut across the school's professions, grades, and subject matter. Like resilient classroom strategies, these reform initiatives are intended to strengthen schooling practices that will contribute to student success and high achievement. Because such school teams have assumed responsibility for the goals and activities that underlie schoolwide reform, they tend to support the principles that underlie the classroom reforms of resilient classrooms.

Finally, teachers and other educators have a pragmatic understanding of the impact of context on students' behavior and their learning. Incidental to their daily work in schools, they observe large numbers of students moving from classrooms to lunchrooms to playgrounds and note the very different ways that students act under such different conditions. Across their years of teaching, they have observed students move from one year's classroom to the next and understand that the same student can behave very differently in a different teacher's classroom. Because of their routine observations of context, the ecological framework underlying resilient classrooms has strong face validity with teachers.

THE UNFAMILIAR

Other features of resilient classrooms may well be less familiar to teachers. For example, schools habitually attribute students' learning, behavior, and emotional problems to disabilities and disturbances within the students. Past practices have emphasized providing students' with remedial services to correct the disabilities, and accommodations to allow them to succeed despite the disabilities. Resilient classroom practitioners break with this tradition by proposing that some of the problems may reside within the classroom context and not within the students.

In schools, responsibility for the mental health of students is traditionally vested within educational specialists—psychologists, counselors, and social workers—and not within teachers. Students with exceptional emotional or behavioral difficulties are provided with supports through individual and small-group counseling activities that often occur outside of the classroom. The provision of these mental health supports is understood to fall outside of the core responsibilities of schools, and schools have relatively few mental health practitioners to address these needs (Adelman & Taylor, 1999; Davis, 1995). In contrast, resilient classroom strategies emphasize natural supports like teachers, friends, and families as the principle source of socioemotional support for students. Like Adelman (1996; Adelman & Taylor, 1999), we believe that schools cannot achieve the vision implied by educational reform if they fail to address the psychosocial needs of children.

Above all else, the goal of schooling has always been to change the student—increasing student achievement, skill mastery, and success. The measure of school success is an increase in the number of students who pass a mastery exam, the average score on a curricular exam, or the number of students who exit with a high school diploma. Resilient classroom strategies suggest that in some cases the route to greater student success is by changing the classrooms. Until now education reform initiatives have not addressed the psychosocial skills that students need to learn so as to work effectively and succeed (Dwyer, 2002).

INTEGRATING RESILIENT CLASSROOMS INTO SCHOOLS

How can the resilient classroom approach be integrated into the fabric of schools so that it becomes one of many threads that are woven together to support student success? Systems change principles suggest that it is first necessary to identify gatekeepers who are the people who have decision-making power, ability to distribute resources, and authority within the system (Curtis & Stollar, 2002). In schools, these typically include the principal but may also include highly influential teachers, school board members, or community leaders. Then, it will be essential to identify stakeholders who will be affected by the change, such as the school's parents and teachers, and devise ways to involve them in planning and decision making from the beginning. An important next step will be to formulate realistic, concrete goals for the broader change process that includes resilient classrooms. Is its purpose to increase student success?—To reduce the number of students served through special programs?—To increase teacher participation in school reform efforts? Finally, it will be useful to anticipate other effects that implementation will have on the school beyond those that are inherent in the resilient classroom approach. For example, will parents want to participate in other aspects of school functioning, and will there be resistance to change from any individual or group?

A very simple way to introduce resilient classrooms into a school is to identify a single teacher who would accept the idea readily and work with that teacher alone. Rather than recruit broadly for a teacher, a consultant could target a teacher who is influential in the building, excited about trying new things, and has effective and innovative teaching strategies that might enrich the classroom change strategies that are planned. The resilient classroom approach appeals to many of the needs that teachers experience but which may go unmet in some schools, such as a sense of community, an avenue for professional growth, and enhanced teaching and management efficacy (Marks, 1995). When presenting the model to a teacher, we briefly summarize the model for classroom resilience and then provide one or two examples of successful classroom change projects. Nothing breeds success like success, and word will spread about resilient classrooms when this early effort is successful.

In many schools, teacher interest in trying new practices is related to perceived support by the principal (Vadasy, Jenkins, Antil, Phillips, & Pool, 1997). Resilient classrooms can be presented to principals by appealing to their concerns for discipline and high achievement scores. Principals appreciate a written proposal that outlines the basic ideas of resilient classrooms, how it directly addresses their goals and concerns, and a plan for how the consultant will support the plan. It is important to explain how the resilient classroom activities fit naturally within the consultant's existing duties and how these will affect other tasks the consultant regularly performs.

Once principals understand how the resilient classroom approach can enhance classroom functioning, they may seize upon it as an opportunity to obtain help for struggling teachers. Consultants should curb this kind of enthusiasm by emphasizing that the consultation strategy will work best when everyone participates voluntarily. Although some struggling teachers may be some of the first to request assistance in their classrooms, others will wait to see if the strategy works before committing themselves to participation in the program. Once resilient classroom projects are underway in one or more classrooms, it will be important to update the principal periodically on the number of classrooms that are receiving services and the general issues being addressed. Care should be taken, however, to keep these reports general so that teacher identity and confidentiality concerning progress are maintained.

A third avenue is to integrate resilient classroom projects into school programs that are already serving children successfully. For examples, schools with strong prereferral student assistance teams can be helped to use classroom-changing rather than student-changing strategies in some instances. Alternatively, the school's accountability or school improvement team could incorporate the resilient classroom approach as a strategy for moving reform efforts down to the classroom level. Resilient classroom practices provide strategies that student assistance teams or school improvement teams can use to tailor their efforts to fit each classroom's unique environment and to involve the people who must interact in that system.

A single consultant working in isolation may end up with more requests for consultation than can be handled effectively by one person. Inevitably, resilient classroom projects will need to become team efforts. Teams can reasonably assume leadership for classroom intervention programs, since the knowledge base that underlies the interventions is cross-disciplinary, the prerequisite skills are not unique to any single profession, and the consultant role is compatible with diverse educational roles. Even with partners sharing the responsibility for classroom changes, it is important that the team not overcommit.

AN EXAMPLE OF SCHOOL CHANGE

A veteran school psychologist was assigned to a bilingual inner-city school that was performing poorly on state standards. The district also assigned a new principal to the building, and allowed the school 3 years to improve the lagging test scores or it would become a charter school. The school psychologist, in collaboration with the principal, invited the teachers to participate in weekly classroom meetings that could enhance students' academic and social goal-setting skills and foster satisfying relationships among students in the class. (The intervention is described in greater detail in Chapter 8.) Through the class meetings, the school psychologist was able to address the state standards, directly support student achievement in the classroom, and model new strategies that teachers could imitate to address students' motivation and interpersonal needs. Just as important, the school psychologist served a broad selection of students throughout the school and the principal was able to participate by reinforcing prosocial behaviors and attainment of students. Teachers responded quite favorably to these suggestions for change, and before long classroom meetings were occurring on a weekly basis in all third- through fifth-grade classrooms. The impact of the intervention on students and teachers was notable. Many teachers held classroom meetings more frequently than once per week because their communications with students improved so dramatically. Students were excited about reaching their own academic and social goals and looked forward to receiving their certificate of accomplishment from the principal. Figure 10.1 is an example of such a certificate. Some students took these home to share with their parents while others posted them in their classrooms or in the hallways.

SUMMARY

This book has proposed a framework for resilient classrooms in which classrooms are assessed, weaknesses in their supports for learning are identified, interventions are systematically planned and implemented, and data are used to assess the impact of the plan. This framework is proposed not as a substitute for current change-the-child strategies for educational intervention but as a supplement to them. Dwyer (2002) has suggested that students' behavior and socialization problems frequently reflect normal responses to irritating factors in the environment rather than emotional conflicts within the child. The resilient classrooms framework provides an alternative form of service delivery that can reduce the irritations. A middle school administrator explained it this way: "It's like a fish bowl. All the other people come into our school and try to fix the fish. You're trying to clean up the water." Cleaning up the water does not always fix the fish, but it's almost impossible to keep the fish healthy until the water is clean.

FIGURE 10.1. Example of an achievement certificate.

Appendix A

ClassMaps Surveys

CLASSMAPS

Directions: The following questions ask what you think is true about your class. Do not put your name on the paper. No one will know what your answers are. For each question, circle the choice that is true for you.

Believing in Me

1. In this class, I understand how to do my work correctly.

   Yes Sometimes No

2. I can do as well as most kids in this class.

   Yes Sometimes No

3. In this class, I understand my work enough to help other kids understand it too.

   Yes Sometimes No

4. My teacher thinks I can do a good job in my work in this class.

   Yes Sometimes No

5. I do not worry about hard work in this class because I know I can do it.

   Yes Sometimes No

6. Other kids in this class know that I do my work well.

   Yes Sometimes No

Taking Charge

7. I want to know more about the things we learn in this class.

   Yes Sometimes No

8. In this class, I help decide what I will learn about.

   Yes Sometimes No

(continued)

9. I can tell when I make mistakes on my work in this class.

   Yes Sometimes No

10. I know what I can do so that I will do well on my work in this class.

    Yes Sometimes No

11. I know how to get help in this class when I need it.

    Yes Sometimes No

12. When the work is hard in this class, I keep trying until I figure it out.

    Yes Sometimes No

13. When something is hard in this class, I try out new ways to learn it.

    Yes Sometimes No

Following the Class Rules

14. I follow the rules in this class.

    Yes Sometimes No

15. I pay attention when I am supposed to in this class.

    Yes Sometimes No

16. I do my work when I am supposed to be working in this class.

    Yes Sometimes No

17. I am careful not to bother other students by moving around or making noises.

    Yes Sometimes No

18. Most kids follow the rules in this class.

    Yes Sometimes No

19. Most kids in this class pay attention when they are supposed to.

    Yes Sometimes No

20. Most kids do their work when they are supposed to in this class.

    Yes Sometimes No

(continued)

21. Most kids work quietly and calmly in this class.

    Yes Sometimes No

My Teacher

22. My teacher listens carefully to me when I talk.

    Yes Sometimes No

23. My teacher helps me when I need help.

    Yes Sometimes No

24. My teacher respects me.

    Yes Sometimes No

25. My teacher believes that I am an important member of this class.

    Yes Sometimes No

26. My teacher makes it fun to be in this class.

    Yes Sometimes No

27. My teacher is fair to me.

    Yes Sometimes No

My Classmates

28. I have a lot of fun with my friends in this class.

    Yes Sometimes No

29. I have a friend to play with at recess.

    Yes Sometimes No

30. I know other kids will not argue with me.

    Yes Sometimes No

31. I have a friend to eat lunch with.

    Yes Sometimes No

(continued)

32. I know other kids will not tease me, call me names, or make fun of me.

    Yes Sometimes No

33. I know other kids will not hit me or push me.

    Yes Sometimes No

34. I have a friend who will stick up for me if someone picks on me.

    Yes Sometimes No

Talking with My Parents

35. I talk with my parents about my grades in this class.

    Yes Sometimes No

36. I talk with my parents about what I am learning in this class.

    Yes Sometimes No

37. I ask my parents for help with homework when I need it.

    Yes Sometimes No

38. I talk with my parents about things I do before and after school.

    Yes Sometimes No

39. I talk with my parents about good things I have done in this class

    Yes Sometimes No

40. I talk with my parents about problems I have in this class like getting in trouble or fights.

    Yes Sometimes No

Appendix B

Worksheets

GOAL-SETTING WORKSHEET

Classroom: ____________________ Date of goal setting: _______________

What strengths are shown by your classroom data?

____

____

____

What weaknesses are shown that you would like to see improve?

____

____

____

Which of these weaknesses is the most important one to change?

____

____

In addition to the classroom data, what other evidence do you have that this weakness is a problem for the class?

____

____

____

What are the times and places when this weakness is particularly a problem for the class?

____

____

____

What are the times and places when this weakness is not present or is not a problem for the class?

____

____

____

(continued)

What else is happening in the class that might be contributing to this weakness? (Examples might include certain individuals who are present, the size of the group, time of day, seating arrangement, expectations for a task, and the degree of structure or last of structure present.)

____

____

____

____

What will the classroom be like once the weakness is "fixed"? This will be the **Classroom Goal**.

____

____

____

____

How will you know if your class meets the goal?

____

____

____

____

What additional data will you collect for your classroom goal?

What data will be collected?

____

Who will collect the data?

____

When and how often?

____

(continued)

Goal-Setting Worksheet *(page 3 of 3)*

Plan for your class meeting

What classroom data would you like to show to the class? (Consider showing one graph reflecting a class strength and a second graph reflecting a class weakness.)

____

____

What questions do you want to ask the class about the data?

- ❑ Does the class think the data are accurate?
- ❑ What do they think the teacher could do differently to make things better?
- ❑ What do they think the students could do to make things better?
- ❑ What else might help make things better?
- ❑ Other questions?

____

____

When should the team meet again?

(By then, the class meeting will have been held, there will be more data, and the team can discuss a plan for class change.)

A good time and date:

____

CLASSROOM MEETING WORKSHEET

Classroom: ______________________ Date of class meeting: ____________

What questions were asked of the class?

- ❑ Do you think the classroom data are accurate?
- ❑ What do you think caused the problem?
- ❑ What do you think the teacher could do differently to make things better?
- ❑ What do you think students could do to make things better?

Did the class think that the classroom data were accurate?

- ❑ Completely inaccurate
- ❑ Kind of inaccurate
- ❑ Neutral
- ❑ Accurate with a few inaccuracies
- ❑ Very accurate

What words did the class use to describe the problem?

____

____

____

____

What did the students think caused the problem?

____

____

____

____

(continued)

Classroom Meeting Worksheet *(page 2 of 2)*

What did the students think they could do to make things better?

____

____

____

____

What did the students think the teacher could do to make things better?

____

____

____

____

INTERVENTION PLANNING WORKSHEET

Classroom: ______________________ Date of planning: _____________

Just a reminder: Your ClassMaps goal

(This is the same as we set in the last meeting.)

____

____

____

What do your baseline data show?

What data were collected?

____

Who collected the data?

____

When and how often?

____

What did the data show?

____

____

____

Do we need to change the plan for data collection?

____

Collecting different data?

____

Change who collects the data?

____

(continued)

When and how often?

____

Planning for change

What new information was learned from the classroom meeting or data collection?

____

____

____

What can be done in this class to reach the goal? Options might include any or all of the following:

❑ Changing classroom routines

____

❑ Changing teacher behaviors

____

❑ Changing student behaviors

____

❑ Increasing teacher skills

____

❑ Changing the physical setting of the playground or other school facilities (by adding things or rearranging existing things)

____

❑ Changing the physical setting of the class (by adding things or rearranging existing things)

____

❑ Modifying classroom discipline procedures

____

❑ Anything else?

____

(continued)

Are there any evidence based interventions that could be used?

____

____

____

The plan

What will be done?

____

____

____

Who will do it?

____

____

When will it be done?

____

____

What data will be kept to show progress toward the goal?

____

____

____

When should we meet again?

(By then, the class plan will have been implemented, we'll have some new information, and we can discuss the plan's progress.)

A good time and date:

____

PLAN RECORD WORKSHEET

Classroom: ____________________ Record for week of: ________________

	Did this happen?
Activity 1 What will be done? ______________________________ ______________________________ ______________________________ Who will do it? ______________________________ When? ______________________________ Where? ______________________________	YES PARTLY NO
Activity 2 What will be done? ______________________________ ______________________________ ______________________________ Who will do it? ______________________________ When? ______________________________ Where? ______________________________	YES PARTLY NO

(continued)

Plan Record Worksheet *(page 2 of 3)*

Activity 3 What will be done? __________ __________ __________ Who will do it? __________ When? __________ Where? __________	YES PARTLY NO
Activity 4 What will be done? __________ __________ __________ Who will do it? __________ When? __________ Where? __________	YES PARTLY NO

(continued)

Plan Record Worksheet *(page 3 of 3)*

What data will be collected? ____

____

Who will collect the data? ____

When and how often? ____

How will the information be recorded? ____________________________

Use this chart to record data as appropriate.

Monday	Tuesday	Wednesday	Thursday	Friday

What did the data show?

____

____

____

Attach the actual data records.

References

Adelman, H. S. (1996). Restructuring educational support services and integrating community resources: Beyond the full service school model. *School Psychology Review, 25,* 431–445.

Adelman, H. S., & Taylor, L. (1990). Intrinsic motivation and school misbehavior: Some intervention implications. *Journal of Learning Disabilities, 23*(9), 541–550.

Adelman, H. S., & Taylor, L. (1999). *School–community partnerships: A guide.* Los Angeles: UCLA, Center for Mental Health in Schools.

American Institutes for Research. (1994). *The AIR Self-Determination Scale.* New York: Columbia University.

American Psychiatric Association. (2000). *Diagnostic and statistical manual of mental disorders* (4th ed., text rev.). Washington, DC: Author.

Ames, C. A. (1990). Motivation: What teachers need to know. *Teachers College Record, 91,* 409–421.

Ames, C. A. (1992a). Achievement goals and the classroom motivational climate. In D. H. Schunk & J. L. Meece (Eds.), *Student perceptions in the classroom* (pp. 327–348). Hillsdale, NJ: Erlbaum.

Ames, C. A. (1992b). Classrooms: goals, structures, and student motivation. *Journal of Educational Psychology, 84,* 261–271.

Asher, S. R. (1995, June). *Children and adolescents with peer relationship problems.* Workshop presented at the Annual Summer Institute in School Psychology: Internalizing Disorders in Children and Adolescents, Denver, CO.

Asher, S. R., & Hymel, S. (1986). Coaching in social skills for children who lack friends in school. *Social Work in Education, 8,* 203–218.

Assor, A., Kaplan, H., & Roth, G. (2002). Choice is good, but relevance is excellent: Autonomy-enhancing and suppressing teacher behaviours predicting students' engagement in schoolwork. *British Journal of Educational Psychology, 72,* 261–278.

Bahr, M. W., Whitten, E., Dieker, L., Kocarek, C., & Manson, D. (1999). A comparison of school-based intervention teams: Implications for education and legal reform. *Exceptional Children, 66,* 67–83.

Baker, J., Terry, T., Bridger, R., & Winsor, A. (1997). Schools as caring communities. *School Psychology Review, 26,* 586–602.

Bandura, A. (1977a). Self-efficacy: Toward a unifying theory of behavioral change. *Psychological Review, 84,* 191–215.

Bandura, A. (1977b). *Social learning theory.* Englewood Cliffs, NJ: Prentice Hall.

Bandura, A. (1986). *Social foundations of thought and action: A social cognitive theory.* Englewood Cliffs, NJ: Prentice Hall.

Bandura, A. (1989). Human agency in cognitive theory. *American Psychologist, 44,* 1175–1184.

Bandura, A. (1993). Perceived self-efficacy in cognitive development and functioning. *Educational Psychologist, 28*(2), 117–148.

Bandura, A. (1997). *Self-efficacy: The exercise of control.* Englewood Cliffs, NJ: Prentice Hall.

Barclay, J. R. (1966). Sociometric choices and teacher ratings as predictors of school dropout. *Journal of Social Psychology, 4,* 40–45.

Barclay, J. R. (1992). Sociometry, temperament and school psychology. In T. R. Kratochwill, S. Elliott, & M. Gettinger (Eds.), *Advances in school psychology* (Vol. 8, pp. 79–114). Hillsdale, NJ: Erlbaum.

Barkley, R. (1997). *Defiant children* (2nd ed.): *A clinician's manual for assessment and parent training.* New York: Guilford Press.

Bear, G. G., Telzrow, C. F., & deOliveira, E. A. (1997). Socially responsible behavior. In G. G. Bear, K. M. Minke, & A. Thomas (Eds.), *Children's needs II: Development, problems and alternatives* (pp. 51–63). Bethesda, MD: National Association of School Psychologists.

Bempechat, J., Graham, S. E., & Jimenez, N. V. (1999). The socialization of achievement in poor and minority students: A comparative study. *Journal of Cross-Cultural Psychology, 30,* 139–158.

Berliner, D. C. (1998, February). *The development of expertise in pedagogy.* Charles W. Hunt memorial lecture presented at the annual meeting of the American Association of Colleges for Teacher Education, New Orleans, LA.

Berndt, T. J. (1981). Effects of friendship on prosocial intentions and behavior. *Child Development, 52,* 636–643.

Berndt, T. J. (1984). Sociometric, socio-cognitive and behavioral measures for the study of friendship and popularity. In T. Field, J. L. Roopnarine, & M. Segal (Eds.), *Friendship in normal and handicapped children* (pp. 31–45). Norwood, NJ: Ablex.

Berndt, T. J. (1999). Friends' influence on students' adjustment to school. *Educational Psychologist, 34,* 15–29.

Berndt, T. J., & Das, R. (1987). Effects of popularity and friendship on perceptions of the personality and social behavior of peers. *Journal of Early Adolescence, 7,* 429–439.

Berndt, T. J., & Perry, T. B. (1986). Children's perceptions of friendships as supportive relationships. *Developmental Psychology, 22,* 640–648.

Blum, R. W., McNeely, C. A., & Rinehart, P. M. (2002). *Improving the odds: The untapped power of schools to improve the health of teens.* Minneapolis: University of Minnesota, Center for Adolescent Health and Development.

Blumenfeld, P. C., Hamilton, V. L., Wessels, K. & Falkner, D. (1979). Teaching responsibility to first graders. *Theory into Practice, 18,* 174–180.

Bouffard-Bouchard, T. (1989). Influence of self-efficacy on performance in a cognitive task. *Journal of Social Psychology, 130,* 353–363.

Boyer, H. (1983). *High school: A report on secondary education in America.* New York: Harper & Row.

Brinker, R. P., & Thorpe, M. E. (1986). Features of integrated educational ecologies that predict social behavior among severely mentally retarded and non-retarded students. *American Journal of Mental Deficiency, 91,* 150–159.

Bronfenbrenner, U. (1979). *The ecology of human development: Experiments by nature and design.* Cambridge, MA: Harvard University Press.

Brophy, J. E. (1987). Synthesis of research on strategies for motivating students to learn. *Educational Leadership, 45,* 40–48.

Brophy, J. E. (1999). Toward a model of the value aspects of motivation in education: Developing appreciation for particular learning domains and activities. *Educational Psychologist, 34,* 75–86.

Brown, D., Pryzwansky, W. B., & Schulte, A. C. (2001). *Psychological consultation: Introduction to theory and practice* (5th ed.). Boston: Allyn & Bacon.

Buhs, E. S., & Ladd, G. W. (2001). Peer rejection as antecedent of young children's school adjustment: An examination of mediating processes. *Developmental Psychology, 37,* 550–560.

Bukowski, W. M., Hoza, B., & Newcomb, A. F. (1994). Using rating scale and nomination techniques to measure friendship and popularity. *Journal of Social and Personal Relationships, 11,* 485–488.

Bullis, M, Walker, H. M., & Sprague, J. R. (2001). A promise unfulfilled: Social skills training with at-risk and antisocial children and youth. *Exceptionality, 9,* 67–90.

Bus, A. G., & van Ijzendoorn, M.H. (1995). Mothers reading to their 3-year-olds: The role of mother–child attachment security in becoming literate. *Reading Research Quarterly,* 30, 998–1015.

Caine, R., & Caine, G. (1994). *Making connections: Teaching and the human brain.* Menlo Park, CA: Addison-Wesley/Innovative Learning.

Camp, B. W., & Bash, M. A. (1980). Think aloud: Improving self-control through training in problem-solving. In D. Rathjen & J. P. Foreyt (Eds.), *Social competence: Intervention for children and adults* (pp. 24–53). Elmsford, NY: Pergamon Press.

Camp, B. W. & Bash, M. A. (1981). *Think aloud: Increasing social and cognitive skills—A problem-solving program for children.* Champaign, IL: Research Press.

Caplan, G. (1963). Types of mental health consultation. *American Journal of Orthopsychiatry, 3,* 470–481.

Caplan, G. (1970). *The theory and practice of mental health consultation.* New York: Basic Books.

Capra, F. (1996). *The web of life.* New York: Doubleday.

Chall, J. S. (2000). *The academic achievement challenge: What really works in the classroom?* New York: Guilford Press.

Chambless, D. L., & Hollon, D. S. (1998). Defining empirically supported therapies. *Journal of Consulting and Clinical Psychology, 66,* 7–18.

Chambless, D. L., Sanderson, W. C., Shoham, V., Johnson, S. B., Pope, K. S., Critis-Cristoph, P., Baker, M., Johnson, B., Woody, S. R., Sue, S., Beutler, L., Williams, D. A., & McCurry, S. (1996). An update on empirically validated therapies. *Clinical Psychologist, 49,* 5–14.

Charlop, M. H., Burgio, L. D., Iwata, B. A., & Ivancic, M. T. (1988). Stimulus variation as a means of enhancing punishment effects. *Journal of Applied Behavior Analysis, 21,* 89–93.

Chaskin, R. J., & Rauner, D. M. (1995). Youth and caring. *Phi Delta Kappan, 76,* 667–679.

Children's Defense Fund. (2002). *The state of children in America's union: A 2002 action guide to leave no child behind.* Washington, DC: Author.

Christenson, S. L., & Anderson, A. R. (2002). Commentary: The centrality of the learning context for students' academic enabler skills. *School Psychology Review, 31,* 378–393.

Christenson, S. L., & Godber, Y. (2001). Enhancing constructive family–school connections. In J. A. Hughes, A. M. LaGreca, & J. C. Conoley (Eds.), *Handbook of psychological services for children and adolescents* (pp. 455–476). Oxford, England: Oxford University Press.

Christenson, S. L. (1995). Supporting home–school collaboration. In A. Thomas & J. Grimes (Eds.), *Best practices in school psychology III* (pp. 253–267). Bethesda, MD: National Association of School Psychologists.

Christenson, S. L., & Peterson, C. J. (1998). *Family, school, and community influences on children's learning: A literature review.* Minneapolis: All Parents Are Teachers Project (formerly Live & Learn), University of Minnesota Extension Service.

Christenson, S. L., Rounds, T., & Gorney, D. (1992). Family factors and student achievement: An avenue to increase students' success. *School Psychology Quarterly, 7,* 178–206.

Christenson, S. L., & Sheridan, S. M. (2001). *Schools and families: Creating essential* connections for learning. New York: Guilford Press.

Clark, M. L. (1991). Social identity, peer relations and academic competence of African-American adolescents. *Education and Urban Society, 24,* 41–52.

Cobb, J. A. (1972). Relationship of discrete classroom behaviors to fourth-grade academic achievement. *Journal of Educational Psychology,* 63, 74–80.

Cobb, J. A., & Hops, H. (1973). Effects of academic survival skills training on low-achieving first graders. *Journal of Educational Research, 67,* 108–113.

Coie, J. D., Dodge, K. A., & Coppotelli, H. (1982). Dimensions and types of social status: A cross-age perspective. *Developmental Psychology, 18,* 557–571.

Coie, J. D., & Krehbiel, G. (1984). Effects of academic tutoring on the social status of low-achieving, socially rejected children. *Child Development,* 55, 1465–1478.

Coie, J. D., & Kupersmidt, J. (1983). A behavior analysis of emerging social status in boys' groups. *Child Development, 54,* 1400–1416.

Coie, J. D., Watt, N. F., West, S. G., Hawkins, J. D., Asarnow, J. R., Markan, H. J., Ramey, S. L., Shure, M., & Long, B. (1993). The science of prevention: A conceptual framework and some directions for a national research program. *American Psychologist, 48,* 1013–1022.

Cole, C. L. (1992). Self-management interventions in the schools. *School Psychology Review, 21,* 188–192.

Cole, C. L., & Bambara, L. M. (1992). Issues surrounding the use of self-management interventions in the schools. *School Psychology Review, 21,* 193–201.

Coleman, J. S., & Schneider, R. B. (1993). *Parents, their children, and schools.* Boulder, CO: Westview Press.

Comer, J. P. (1993). *School power: Implications of an intervention project.* New York: Free Press.

Comer, J. P., Haynes, N. M., & Joyner, E. T. (1996). The School Development Program. In J. P. Comer, N. M. Haynes, E. T. Joyner, & M. Ben-Avie (Eds.), *Rallying the whole village: The Comer process for reforming education* (pp. 1–26). New York: Teachers College Press.

Comer, J. P., Haynes, N. M., Joyner, E. T., & Ben-Avie, M. (Eds.). (1996). *Rallying the whole village: The Comer process for reforming education.* New York: Teachers College Press.

Committee for Children. (1992). *Second Step: A violence prevention curriculum.* Seattle, WA: Author.

Connell, J. P., & Wellborn, J. G. (1991). Competence, autonomy, and relatedness: A motivational analysis of self-system processes. In M. R. Gunnar & L. A. Sroufe (Eds.), *Minnesota Symposia on Child Development: Vol. 23. Self processes and development* (pp. 43–78). Hillsdale, NJ: Erlbaum.

Conoley, C. W., Conoley, J. C., Ivey, D. C., & Scheel, M. J. (1991). Enhancing consultation by matching the consultee's perspectives. *Journal of Counseling and Development, 69,* 546–549.

Conoley, J. C., & Conoley, C. W. (1992). *School consultation: Practice and training* (2nd ed.). Boston: Allyn & Bacon.

Covington, M. V. (1992). *Making the grade: A self-worth perspective on motivation and school reform.* New York: Cambridge University Press.

Cowen, E. L. (1994). The enhancement of psychological wellness: Challenges and opportunities. *American Journal of Community Psychology, 22,* 148–180.

Cowen, E. L., Hightower, A. D., Pedro-Carroll, J. L., Work, W. C., Wyman, P. A., & Haffey, W. G. (1996). *School-based prevention for children at risk: The primary mental health project.* Washington, DC: American Psychological Association.

Curtis, M. J., & Stollar, S. A. (2002). Best practices in system-level change. In A. Thomas & J. Grimes (Eds.), *Best practices in school psychology IV* (pp. 223–234). Bethesda, MD: National Association of School Psychologists.

Davis, W. E. (1995). Full-service schools for youth at risk: Overcoming obstacles to effective implementation. *Journal of At-Risk Issues, 2,* 11–17.

Deci, E. L., Hodges, R., Pierson, L., & Tomassone, J. (1992). Autonomy and competence as motivational factors in students with learning disabilities and emotional handicaps. *Journal of Learning Disabilities, 25,* 457–471.

Deci, E. L., Nezlek, J., & Sheinman, L. (1981). Characteristics of the rewarder and intrinsic motivation of the rewardee. *Journal of Personality and Social Psychology, 40,* 1–10.

Deci, E. L., & Ryan, R. M. (1985). *Intrinsic motivation and self-determination in human behavior.* New York: Plenum Press.

Deno, S. L. (1985). Curriculum-based measurement: The emerging alternative. *Exceptional Children, 52,* 219–232.

Deno, S. L. (2002). Problem solving as "best practice." In A. Thomas & J. Grimes (Eds.), *Best practices in school psychology IV* (pp. 37–55). Bethesda, MD: National Association of School Psychologists.

Deno, S. L., Fuchs, L. S., Marston, D., & Shin, J. (2001). Using curriculum-based measurement to establish growth standards for students with learning disabilities. *School Psychology Review, 30,* 507–524.

Developmental Studies Center. (1996). *Ways we want our class to be: Class meetings that build commitment to kindness and learning.* Oakland, CA: Author.

Doll, B. (1996). Children without friends: Implications for practice and policy. *School Psychology Review, 25,* 165–183.

Doll, B., Acker, P., Goalstone, J., McLain, J., & Zubia, V., with Chavez, M., Griffin, J., & Hickman, A. (2000). Cohesion and dissension in a multi-agency family service team: A qualitative examination of service integration. *Children's Services: Social Policy, Research and Practice, 3,* 1–21.

Doll, B., & Doll, C. (1997). *Bibliotherapy with young people: Librarians and mental health professionals working together.* Englewood, CO: Libraries Unlimited.

Doll, B., & Elliott, S. R. (1994). Representativeness of observed preschool social behaviors: How much data is enough? *Journal of Early Intervention, 18,* 227–238.

Doll, B., & Lyon, M. (1998). Risk and resilience: Implications for the practice of school psychology. *School Psychology Review, 27,* 348–363.

Doll, B., Siemers, E. E., & Brey, K. (2003, August). *ClassMaps consultation: An ecological measurement of successful classroom contexts.* Poster presented at the annual meeting of the American Psychological Association, Toronto, Ontario.

Doll, B., Siemers, E., Song, S., & Nickolite, A. (2002). *ClassMaps consultation: A step-by-step manual.* Unpublished manuscript.

Doll, B., Zucker, S., & Brehm, K. (1999a, April). *Reliability and validity of ClassMaps.* Poster presentation at the annual meeting of the National Association of School Psychologists, Las Vegas, NV. (ERIC Document Reproduction Services No. ED 435 934)

Doll, B., Zucker, S., & Brehm, K. (1999b, September). *ClassMaps in urban settings: Improving the social and academic quality of classrooms.* Workshop presented at the National Conference on School-Based Mental Health Services, Denver, CO.

Dweck, C. S., & Leggett, E. L. (1988). A social-cognitive approach to motivation and personality. *Psychological Review, 95,* 256–273.

Dwyer, K. P. (2002). Mental health in the schools. *Journal of Child and Family Studies, 11,* 101–111.

Eccles, J. S., Midgley, C., Wigfield, A., Buchanan, C. M., Reuman, D., Flanagan, C., & MacIver, D. (1993). Development during adolescence: The impact of stage–environment fit on young adolescents' experiences in schools and in families. *American Psychologist, 48,* 90–101.

Eccles, J., Wigfield, A., Harold, R. D., & Blumenfeld, P. (1993). Age and gender differences in children's self- and task perceptions during elementary school. *Child Development, 64,* 830–847.

Eddy, J. M., Reid, J. B., & Fetrow, R. A. (2000). An elementary school-based prevention program targeting modifiable antecedents of youth delinquency and violence: Linking the Interests of Families and Teachers (LIFT). *Journal of Emotional and Behavioral Disorders, 8,* 165–176.

Elias, M. J. (2003). *Academic and social-emotional learning.* Brussels: International Academy of Education.

Elias, M. J., & Tobias, S. E. (1996). *Social problem solving: Interventions in the schools.* New York: Guilford Press.

Elias, M. J., Zins, J., Weissberg, R., Frey, K., Greenberg, M., Haynes, N., Kessler, R. Schwab-Stone, M., & Shriver, T. (1997). *Promoting social and emotional learning.* Alexandria, VA: Association for Supervision and Curriculum Development.

Elliott, S. N. (1988). Acceptability of behavioral treatments in educational settings. In J. C. Witt, S. N. Elliott, & F. M. Gresham (Eds.), *The handbook of behavior therapy in education* (pp. 121–150). New York: Plenum Press.

Elliott, S. N., & Von Brock Treuting, M. (1991). The Behavior Intervention Rating Scale: Development and validation of a pretreatment acceptability and effectiveness measure. *Journal of School Psychology, 29,* 43–52.

Epstein, J. (1995, May). School, family, community partnerships: Caring for the children we share. *Phi Delta Kappan, 77*(9), 701–712.

Erchul, W. P. (1987). A relational communication analysis of control in school consultation. *Professional School Psychology, 2,* 113–124.

Estrada, P., Arsenio, W. F., Hess, R., & Holloway, S. (1987). Affective quality of the mother–child relationship: Longitudinal consequences for the child's school-relevant cognitive functioning. *Developmental Psychology, 23,* 210–215.

Faber, A., & Mazlish, E. (1995). *How to talk so kids can learn.* New York: Rawson Associates.

Fantuzzo, J. W., & Rohrbeck, C. A. (1992). Self-managed groups: Fitting self-management approaches into classroom systems. *School Psychology Review, 21,* 255–263.

Fehrmann, P. G., Keith, T. Z., & Reimers, T. M. (1987). Home influences on school learning: Direct and indirect effects of parent involvement on high school grades. *Journal of Educational Research, 80,* 330–337.

Feigelson, S. (1998). *Energize your meetings with laughter.* Alexandria, VA: Association for Supervision and Curriculum Development.

Finn, J. D. (1993). *School engagement and students at risk.* Washington, DC: U.S. Department of Education, National Center for Educational Statistics.

Finn, J. D. (1998). Parental engagement that makes a difference. *Educational Leadership, 55,* 20–24.

Fish, M. C., & Dane, E. (2000). The Classroom Systems Observation Scale: Development of an instrument to assess classrooms using a systems perspective. *Learning Environments Research, 3,* 67–92.

Fluegelman, A. (1976). *The new games book.* Garden City, NY: Doubleday Press.

Flugum, K., & Reschly, D. (1994). Prereferral interventions: Quality indices and outcomes. *Journal of School Psychology, 32,* 1–14.

Friend, M., & Cook, L. (1997). Student-centered teams in schools: Still in search of an identity. *Journal of Educational and Psychological Consultation, 8,* 3–20.

Fuchs, D., Fuchs, L.S., & Bahr, M. (1990). Mainstream assistance teams: A scientific basis for the art of consultation. *Exceptional Children, 57,* 128–139.

Garrity, C., Jens, K., Porter, W., Sager, N., & Short-Camilli, C. (2000). *Bully-proofing your school: A comprehensive approach for elementary schools.* Boulder, CO: Sopris West.

Gass, M. A. (1995). *Book of metaphors.* Dubuque, IA: Kendall/Hunt.

Gettinger, M. (1986). Issues and trends in academic engaged time of students. *Special Services in the Schools, 2,* 1–17.

Glasser, W. (1969). *Schools without failure.* New York: Harper & Row.

Goldstein, A. P. (1999). *The prepare curriculum.* Champaign, IL: Research Press.

Good, T. L., & Brophy, J. E. (1987). *Looking in classrooms* (4th ed.). New York: Harper & Row.

Greenberg, M. T., Kusche, C., & Mihalic, S. F. (1998). *Blueprints for violence prevention: Promoting alternative thinking strategies.* Boulder: University of Colorado, Institute of Behavioral Science, Center for the Study and Prevention of Violence.

Greenwood, C. R., Delquadri, J. C., & Hall, R. V. (1989). Longitudinal effects of classwide peer tutoring. *Journal of Educational Psychology, 81*(3), 371–383.

Greenwood, C. R., Maheady, L., & Delquadri, J. C. (2002). Classwide peer tutoring programs. In M. R. Shinn, H. M. Walker, & G. Stoner (Eds.), *Interventions for academic and behavior problems II: Preventive and remedial approaches* (pp. 611–649). Bethesda, MD: National Association of School Psychologists.

Gresham, F. M. (1986). Conceptual issues in the assessment of social competence in children. In P. Strain, M. Guralnick, & H. Walker (Eds.), *Children's social behavior: Development, assessment and modification* (pp. 143–180). New York: Academic Press.

Gresham, F. M. (1989). Assessment of treatment integrity in school consultation and prereferral intervention. *School Psychology Review, 18,* 37–50.

Gresham, F. M. (2002). Best practices in social skills training. In A. Thomas & J. Grimes (Eds.), *Best practices in school psychology IV* (pp. 1029–1040). Bethesda, MD: National Association of School Psychologists.

Gresham, F. M., Sugai, C., & Horner, R. H. (2001). Interpreting outcomes of social skills training for students with high-incidence disabilities. *Exceptional Children, 67,* 331–344.

Grolnick, W. S., Kurowski, C. O., & Gurland, S. T. (1999). Family processes and the development of children's self-regulation. *Educational Psychologist, 34,* 3–14.

Grolnick, W. S., & Ryan, R. M. (1987). Autonomy in children's learning: An experimental and individual difference investigation. *Journal of Personality and Social Psychology, 52,* 890–898.

Hamre, B. K., & Pianta, R. C. (2001). *STARS: Students, teachers and relationship support.* Lutz, FL: Psychological Assessment Resources.

Harackiewicz, J. M., Manderlink, G., & Sansone, C. (1992). Competence processes and achievement motivation: Implications for intrinsic motivation. In A. K. Boggiano & T. S. Pittman (Eds.), *Achievement and motivation: A social-developmental perspective* (pp. 115–137). Cambridge, England: Cambridge University Press.

Hartman, W. T., & Fay, T. A. (1996). Cost-effectiveness of instructional support teams in Pennsylvania. *Journal of Educational Finance, 21,* 555–580.

Heller, K., & Swindle, R. W. (1983). Social networks, perceived social support and coping with stress. In R. D. Felner, L. A. Jason, J. N. Mortisugu, & S. S. Farber (Eds.), *Preventive psychology* (pp. 87–103). Elmsford, NY: Pergamon Press.

Henderson, N., & Milstein, M. (1996). *Resiliency in schools.* Thousand Oaks, CA: Corwin Press.

Higgins, C. (1994). Improving the school ground environment as an anti-bullying intervention. In P. K. Smith & S. Sharp (Eds.), *School bullying: Insights and perspectives* (pp. 213–244). London: Routledge.

Hollinger, J. D. (1987). Social skills for behaviorally disordered children as preparation for mainstreaming: Theory, practice and new directions. *Remedial and Special Education, 8,* 17–27.

Hoover-Dempsey, K. V., Basler, O. C., & Burow, R. (1995). Parents' reported involvement in students' homework: Strategies and practices. *Elementary School Journal, 95,* 435–450.

Hops, H., & Cobb, J. A. (1974). Initial investigations into academic survival-skill training, direct instruction, and first-grade achievement. *Journal of Educational Psychology, 66,* 548–553.

Hoza, B., Molina, B. S. G., Bukowski, W. M., & Sippola, L. K. (1995). Peer variables as predictors of later childhood adjustment. *Development and Psychopathology, 7,* 787–802.

Illinois State Board of Education. (1994). Parent Involvement Inventory. Available: *http://www.ncrel.org/sdrs/areas/issues/envrnmnt/famncomm/pa4lk12.htm.*

Jacklin, C. N. (1989). Female and male: Issues of gender. *American Psychologist, 44,* 127–133.

Jayanthi, M., & Friend, M. (1992). Interpersonal problem solving: A selective literature review to guide practice. *Journal of Educational and Psychological Consultation, 3,* 39–53.

Jenson, W. R., Rhode, G., & Reavis, H. K. (1994). *The tough kid tool box.* Longmont, CO: Sopris West.

Jinks, J., & Morgan, V. (1999). Children's perceived academic efficacy: An inventory scale. *Clearing House, 72,* 224–231.

Johnson, D. W., Johnson, R. T., & Anderson, D. (1983). Social interdependence and classroom climate. *Journal of Psychology, 114,* 135–142.

Katz, D., & Kahn, R. L. (1978). *The social psychology of organizations* (2nd ed.). New York: Wiley.

Kazdin, A. E. (1975). *Behavior modification in applied settings.* Homewood, IL: Dorsey Press.

Kazdin, A. E. (1982). Single-case experimental designs in clinical research and practice. *New Directions for Methodology of Social and Behavioral Science, 13,* 33–47.

Kendall, P. C., & Bartel, N. R. (1990). *Teaching problem solving to students with learning and behavior problems: A manual for teachers.* Ardmore, PA: Workbook Publishing.

Kendall, P. C., & Braswell, L. (1985). *Cognitive-behavioral therapy for impulsive children.* New York: Guilford Press.

Kiresuk, T. J., Smith, A., & Cardillo, J. E. (1994). *Goal attainment scaling: Applications, theory and measurement.* Hillsdale, NJ: Erlbaum.

Koplow, L. (2002). *Creating schools that heal.* New York: Teachers College Press.

Kounin, J. S. (1970). *Discipline and group management in classrooms.* New York: Holt, Rinehart & Winston.

Kovaleski, J. F. (2002). Best practices in operating pre-referral intervention teams. In A. Thomas & J. Grimes (Eds.), *Best practices in school psychology IV* (pp. 645–655). Bethesda, MD: National Association of School Psychologists.

Kovaleski, J. F., Tucker, J. A., & Stevens, L. (1996). Bridging special education and regular education: The Pennsylvania initiative. *Educational Leadership, 53,* 44–47.

Kupersmidt, J., Coie, J., & Dodge, K. (1990). The role of poor peer relationships in the development of disorder. In S. R. Asher & J. D. Coie (Eds.), *Peer rejection in childhood* (pp. 274–308). Cambridge, England: Cambridge University Press.

Ladd, G. W., & Oden, S. L. (1979). The relationship between peer acceptance and children's ideas about helpfulness. *Child Development, 50,* 402–408.

Ladd, G. W., & Price, J. M. (1987). Predicting children's social and school adjustment following the transition from preschool to kindergarten. *Child Development, 58,* 1168–1189.

Lazarus, B. D. (1993). Self-management and achievement of students with behavior disorders. *Psychology in the Schools, 30,* 67–74.

Locke, E. A., & Latham, G. P. (2002). Building a practically useful theory of goal setting and task motivation: A 35-year odyssey. *American Psychologist, 57*(9), 705–717.

Logan, K. R., Bakeman, R., & Keefe, E. B. (1997). Effects of instructional variables on engaged behavior of students with disabilities in general education classrooms. *Exceptional Children, 63,* 481–497.

Lonigan, C. J., Elbert, J. C., & Bennett-Johnson, S. (1998). Empirically supported psychosocial interventions for children: An overview. *Journal of Clinical Child Psychology, 27,* 138–145.

Luellen, W. S. (2003, February). The effectiveness of social skills training for children with disturbed peer relationships: A review of meta-analyses. *NASP Communiqué, 31*(5), 38–39.

Malecki, C. K., & Elliott, S. N. (2002). Children's social behaviors as predictors of academic achievement. *School Psychology Quarterly, 17,* 1–23.

Marks, E. S. (1995). *Entry strategies for school consultation.* New York: Guilford Press.

Masten, A. S. (2001). Ordinary magic: Resilience processes in development. *American Psychologist, 56,* 227–238.

Masten, A. S., & Coatsworth, J. D. (1998). The development of competence in favorable and unfavorable environments: Lessons from research on successful children. *American Psychologist, 53,* 205–220.

Masten, A. S., Hubbard, J. J., Gest, S. D., Tellegen A., Garmezy, N., & Ramirez, M. (1999). Competence in the context of adversity: Pathways to resilience and maladaptation from childhood to late adolescence. *Development and Psychopathology, 11,* 143–169.

Mathur, S. R., Kavale, K. A., Quinn, M. M., Forness, S. R., & Rutherford, R. B., Jr. (1998). Social skills interventions with students with emotional and behavioral problems: A quantitative synthesis of single-subject research. *Behavioral Disorders, 23,* 193–201.

McDermott, P. A., Mordell, M., & Stoltzfus, J. (2001). The organization of student performance in American schools: Discipline, motivation, verbal learning, and nonverbal learning. *Journal of Educational Psychology, 93*(1), 65–76.

McGinnis, E., & Goldstein, A. P. (2000). *Skillstreaming the elementary school child: New strategies and perspectives for teaching prosocial skills.* Champaign, IL: Research Press.

McNamara, K. (2002). Best practices in promotion of social competence. In A. Thomas & J. Grimes (Eds.), *Best practices in school psychology IV* (pp. 911–928). Bethesda, MD: National Association of School Psychologists.

Meece, L. J., & Courney, D. P. (1992). Gender differences in students' perceptions: Consequences for achievement-related choices. In D. H. Schunk & J. L. Meece (Eds.), *Student perceptions in the classroom* (pp. 209–228). Hillsdale, NJ: Erlbaum.

Metcalf, L. (1995). *Counseling toward solutions: A practical solution-focused program for working with students, teachers, and parents.* West Nyack, NY: Center for Applied Research in Education.

Meyers, B., Valentino, C. T., Meyers, J., Boretti, M., & Brent, D. (1996). Implementing prereferral intervention teams as an approach to school-based consultation in an urban school system. *Journal of Educational and Psychological Consultation, 7,* 119–149.

Middleton, M. J., & Midgley, C. (2002). Beyond motivation: Middle school students' perceptions of press for understanding in math. *Contemporary Educational Psychology, 27,* 373–391.

Miserandino, M. (1996). Children who do well in school: Individual differences in perceived competence and autonomy in above-average children. *Journal of Educational Psychology, 88,* 203–215.

Mitchem, K. J., Young, K. R., West, R. P., & Benyo, J. (2001). CWPASM: A Classwide Peer-Assisted Self-Management Program for general education classrooms. *Education and Treatment of Children, 24,* 111–141.

Multon, K. D., Brown, S. D., & Lent, R. W. (1991). Relation of self-efficacy beliefs to academic outcomes: A meta-analytic investigation. *Journal of Counseling Psychology, 18,* 30–38.

Mulvey, E. P. & Cauffman, E. (2001). The inherent limits of predicting school violence. *American Psychologist, 56,* 797–802.

Murphy, J. J. (1997). *Solution-focused counseling in middle and high schools.* Alexandria, VA: American Counseling Association.

Murphy, P. S. (2002). *The effect of classroom meetings on the reduction of recess problems: A single case design.* Unpublished doctoral dissertation, University of Denver, Denver, CO.

Narayan, J. S., Heward, W. L., Gardner, R., Courson, F. H., & Omness, C. K. (1990). Using response cards to increase student participation in an elementary classroom. *Journal of Applied Behavior Analysis, 21,* 483–490.

National Center for Educational Statistics. (1992). *Tech. Rep. No. NCES 92-042.* Washington, DC: U.S. Government Printing Office.

National Parent–Teacher Association. (1997). *National standards for parent/family involvement programs.* Chicago: Author.

Newcomb, A. F., & Bukowski, W. M. (1984). A longitudinal study of the utility of social preference and social impact sociometric classification schemes. *Child Development, 55,* 1434–1447.

Noblit, G. W., Dwight, L. R., & McCadden, B. M. (1995). In the meantime: The possibilities of caring. *Phi Delta Kappan, 76,* 680–684.

Noddings, N. (1988). Schools face crisis in caring. *Education Week, 8*(14), 32.

Noddings, N. (1992). *The challenge to care in schools: An alternative approach to education.* New York: Teachers College Press.

Olweus, D., Limber, S., & Mihalic, S. F. (1999). *Blueprints for violence prevention, book nine: Bullying prevention program.* Longmont, CO: Center for the Study and Prevention of Violence.

Osterman, K. F. (2000). Students' need for belonging in the school community. *Review of Educational Research, 70,* 323–367.

Pajares, F., & Johnson, M. J. (1996). Self-efficacy beliefs and the writing performance of entering high school students. *Psychology in the Schools, 33,* 163–175.

Pajares, F., & Miller, M. D. (1994). The role of self-efficacy and self-concept beliefs in mathematical problem-solving: A path analysis. *Journal of Educational Psychology, 86,* 193–203.

Paris, S., Byrnes, J. P., & Paris, A. H. (2001). Constructing theories, identities and actions of self-regulated learners. In B. J. Zimmerman & D. H. Schunk (Eds.), *Self-regulated learning and academic achievement: Theoretical perspectives* (pp. 253–287). Mahwah, NJ: Erlbaum.

Parker, J. G., & Asher, S. R. (1989, April). *Peer relations and social adjustment: Are friendship and group acceptance distinct domains?* Paper presented at the biennial meeting of the Society for Research in Child Development, Kansas City, MO.

Parker, J. G., & Asher, S. R. (1993). Friendship and friendship quality in middle childhood: Links with peer group acceptance and feelings of loneliness and social dissatisfaction. *Developmental Psychology, 29,* 611–621.

Patrick, H., Hicks, L., & Ryan, A. M. (1997). Relations of perceived social efficacy and social goal pursuit to self-efficacy for academic work. *Journal of Early Adolescence, 17,* 109–128.

Patrikakou, E. N., & Weissberg, R. P. (2000). Parents' perception of teacher outreach and parent involvement in children's education. *Journal of Prevention and Intervention in the Community, 20,* 103–119.

Pellegrini, A. D. (2002). Rough-and-tumble play from childhood through adolescence: Development and possible functions. In P. K. Smith & C. H. Hart (Eds.), *Blackwell handbook of childhood social development* (pp. 437–453). Malden, MA: Blackwell.

Peña, D. C. (2000). Parent Involvement: Influencing factors and implications. *Journal of Educational Research, 94,* 42–54.

Phelan, P., Yu, H. C., & Davidson, A. L. (1994). Navigating the psychosocial pressures of adolescence: The voices and experiences of high school youth. *American Educational Research Journal, 31,* 415–447.

Pianta, R. C. (1999). *Enhancing relationships between children and teachers.* Washington DC: American Psychological Association.

Pianta, R. C. (2001a). *Student–Teacher Relationship Scale.* Lutz, FL: Psychological Assessment Resources.

Pianta, R. C. (2001b). Implications of a developmental systems model for preventing and treating behavioral disturbances in children and adolescents. In J. A. Hughes, A. M. LaGreca, & J. C. Conoley (Eds.), *Handbook of psychological services for children and adolescents* (pp 23–41). Oxford, England: Oxford University Press.

Pianta, R. C., & Hamre, B. K. (2001). *STARS: Students, Teachers and Relationship Support—Consultant's manual.* Lutz, FL: Psychological Assessment Resources.

Pianta, R C., & Walsh, D. J. (1996). *High-risk children in schools: Constructing sustaining relationships.* New York: Routledge.

Pintrich, P. R. (2000). Multiple goals, multiple pathways: The role of goal orientation in learning and achievement. *Journal of Educational Psychology,* 92(3), 544–555.

Pintrich, P. R., & DeGroot, E. (1990). Motivational and self-regulated learning components of classroom academic performance. *Educational Psychology, 82,* 33–40.

Pintrich, P. R., Roeser, R. W., & DeGroot, E. V. (1994). Classroom and individual differences in early adolescents' motivation and self-regulated learning. *Journal of Early Adolescence, 14,* 139–161.

Pintrich, P. R., & Schunk, D. H. (1996). *Motivation in education: Theory, research, and applications.* Englewood Cliffs, NJ: Merrill/Prentice Hall.

President's Commission on Excellence in Special Education. (2002). *A new era: Revitalizing special education for children and their families.* Washington, DC: U.S. Department of Education.

Pryzwansky, W. B., & White, G. W. (1983). The influence of consultee characteristics on preferences for consultation approaches. *Professional Psychology: Research and Practice, 14,* 457–461.

Quinn, M. M., Kavale, K. A., Mathur, S. R., Rutherford, R. B., Jr., & Forness, S. R. (1999). A meta-analysis of social skill interventions for students with emotional or behavioral disorders. *Journal of Emotional and Behavioral Disorders, 7,* 54–64.

Quinn, M. M., Osher, D., Hoffman, C. C., & Hanley, T. V. (1998). *Safe, drug-free, and effective schools for all students: What works!* Washington, DC: Center for Effective Collaboration and Practice at the American Institutes for Research.

Randi, J., & Corno, L. (2000). Teacher innovations in self-regulated learning. In M. Boekaerts, P. R. Pintrich, & M. Zeidner (Eds.), *Handbook of self-regulation* (pp. 651–685). New York: Academic Press.

Renshaw, P. D., & Asher, S. R. (1983). Children's goals and strategies for social interaction. *Merrill–Palmer Quarterly, 29,* 353–374.

Reynolds, C. R., & Kamphaus, R. W. (1992). *The Behavior Assessment System for Children.* Circle Pines, MN: American Guidance Service.

Rhode, G., Jensen, W., & Reavis, H. K. (1994). *The tough kid book: Practical classroom management strategies.* Longmont, CO: Sopris West.

Ridley, D. S., & Walther, B. (1995). *Creating responsible learners: The role of a positive classroom environment.* Washington, DC: American Psychological Association.

Rohnke, K., & Butler, S. (1997). *Quicksilver: Adventure games, initiative problems, trust activities and a guide to effective leadership.* Dubuque, IA: Kendall/Hunt.

Rosenfield, S. (1992). Developing school-based consultation teams. *School Psychology Quarterly, 7,* 22–46

Ross, D. (1996). *Childhood bullying and teasing: What school personnel, other professionals, and parents can do.* Alexandria, VA: American Counseling Association.

Rumberger, R. W. (1995). Dropping out of middle school: A multilevel analysis of students and schools. *American Educational Research Journal, 32,* 583–625.

Rutter, M. (1985). Resilience in the face of adversity: Protective factors and resistance to psychiatric disorder. *British Journal of Psychiatry, 147,* 598–611.

Rutter, M. (1987). Psychosocial resilience and protective mechanisms. *American Journal of Orthopsychiatry, 37,* 317–331.

Ryan, A. M., Gheen, M. H., & Midgley, C. (1998). Why do some students avoid asking for help?: An examination of the interplay among students' academic efficacy, teachers' social-emotional role, and the classroom goal structure. *Journal of Educational Psychology, 90,* 528–535.

Ryan, A. M., & Pintrich, P. R. (1997). "Should I ask for help?": The role of motivation and attitudes in adolescents' help seeking in math class. *Journal of Educational Psychology, 89*(2), 329–341.

Ryan, R. M., Connell, J. P., & Deci, E. L. (1985). A motivational analysis of self-determination and self-regulation in education. In C. Ames & R. Ames (Eds.), *Research on motivation in education* (Vol. 2, pp. 13–51). San Diego, CA: Academic Press.

Safer, D. J. (1986). Nonpromotion correlates and outcomes at different grade levels. *Journal of Learning Disabilities, 19,* 500–503.

Salisbury, C., Gallucci, C., Palombaro, M. M., & Peck, C. A. (1995). Strategies that promote social relations among elementary students with and without severe disabilities in inclusive schools. *Exceptional Children, 62,* 125–137.

Salomon, G. (1984). Television is "easy" and print is "tough": The differential investment of mental effort in learning as a function of perceptions and attributions. *Journal of Educational Psychology, 76,* 647–658.

Sameroff, A. (1975). Transactional models in early social relations. *Human Development, 18,* 65–79.

Sattes, B. (1985). *Parent involvement: A review of the literature* (Rep. No. 21). Charleston, WV: Appalachia Educational Laboratory.

Schonert-Reichl, K. A. (1993). Empathy and social relationships in adolescents with behavioral disorders. *Behavior Disorders, 18,* 189–204.

Schorr, L. (1988). *Within our reach: Breaking the cycle of disadvantage.* New York: Anchor Books.

Schorr, L. (1997). *Common purpose: Strengthening families and neighborhoods to rebuild America.* New York: Doubleday.

Schunk, D. H. (1983). Reward contingencies and the development of children's skills and self-efficacy. *Journal of Educational Psychology, 75,* 511–518.

Schunk, D. H. (1987). Peer models and children's behavioral change. *Review of Educational Research, 57,* 149–174.

Schunk, D. H. (1989a). Self-efficacy and cognitive achievement: Implications for students with learning problems. *Journal of Learning Disabilities, 22*(1), 14–22.

Schunk, D. H. (1989b). Social cognitive theory and self-regulated learning. In B. J. Zimmerman & D. H. Schunk (Eds.), *Self-regulated learning and academic achievement: Theory, research, and practice* (pp. 83–110). New York: Springer-Verlag.

Schunk, D. H. (1991). Self-efficacy and academic motivation. *Educational Psychologist, 26,* 207–231.

Schunk, D. H., & Zimmerman, B. J. (1997). Social origins of self-regulatory competence. *Educational Psychologist, 32,* 195–208.

Sharp, S., & Smith, P. K. (1994). *School bullying: Insights and perspectives.* New York: Routledge.

Sheridan, S. M. (1997). Conceptual and empirical bases of conjoint behavioral consultation. *School Psychology Quarterly, 12,* 119–133.

Sheridan, S. M., Eagle, J. W., Cowan, R. J., & Mickelson, W. (2001). The effects of conjoint behavioral consultation: Results of a four-year investigation. *Journal of School Psychology, 39,* 361–388.

Sheridan, S. M., & Steck, M. (1995). Acceptability of conjoint behavioral consultation: A national survey of school psychologists. *School Psychology Review, 24,* 633–647.

Shure, M. B. (2001). What's right with prevention?: Commentary on "Prevention of mental disorders in school-aged children: Current state of the field." *Prevention and Treatment, 4,* np.

Shure, M. B., & Spivac, G. (1980). Interpersonal problem solving as a mediator of behavioral adjustment in preschool and kindergarten children. *Journal of Applied Developmental Psychology, 1,* 29–44.

Shure, M. B., & Spivac, G. (1982). Interpersonal problem solving in young children: A cognitive approach to prevention. *American Journal of Community Psychology, 10,* 341–355.

Sieber, R. T. (1979). Classmates as workmates: Informal peer activity in the elementary school. *Anthropology and Education Quarterly, 10,* 207–235.

Siegel, R. G., Galassi, J. P., & Ware, W. B. (1985). A comparison of two models for predicting mathematics performance: Social learning versus math aptitude–anxiety. *Journal of Counseling Psychology, 32,* 531–538.

Sinclair, M. F, Christenson, S. L., Hurley, C., & Evelo, D. (1998). Dropout prevention for high-risk youth with disabilities: Efficacy of a sustained school engagement procedure. *Exceptional Children, 65,* 7–21.

Skinner, E. A. (1996). A guide to constructs of control. *Journal of Personality and Social Psychology, 71,* 549–570.

Slavin, R. E., & Madden, N. A. (2001). *Success for all: Research and reform in elementary education.* Mahwah, NJ: Erlbaum.

Squires, D. A., & Joyner, E. T. (1996). Time and alignment: Potent tools for improving achievement. In J. P. Comer, N. M. Haynes, E. T. Joyner, & M. Ben-Avie (Eds.), *Rallying the whole village: The Comer process for reforming education* (pp. 98–122). New York: Teachers College Press.

Steinberg, L. (1996). *Beyond the classroom.* New York: Touchstone.

Stevens, K. B., Blackhurst, A. E., & Slaton, D. B. (1991). Teaching memorized spelling with a microcomputer: Time delay and computer-assisted instruction. *Journal of Applied Behavior Analysis, 24,* 153–160.

Stevenson, R. B., & Ellsworth, J. (1993). Dropouts and the silencing of critical voices. In L. Weis & M. Fine (Eds.), *Beyond silenced voices: Class, race, and gender in United States schools* (pp. 259–271). Albany: State University of New York Press.

Sugai, G., & Horner, R. (2001, June). *School climate and discipline: Going to scale.* Paper presented at the National Summit on the Shared Implementation of IDEA, Washington DC.

Sugai, G., Horner, R. H., & Gresham, F. M. (2002). Behaviorally effective school environments. In M. R. Shinn, H. M. Walker, & G. Stoner (Eds.), *Interventions for academic and behavior problems II: Preventive and remedial approaches* (pp. 315–350). Bethesda, MD: National Association of School Psychologists.

Sui-Chu, E. H., & Willms, J. D. (1996). Effects of parental involvement on eight-grade achievement. *Sociology of Education, 69,* 126–141.

Telzrow, C. F., McNamara, K., & Hollinger, C. L. (2000). Fidelity of problem-solving implementation and relationship to student performance. *School Pychology Review, 29,* 443–461.

Tollefson, N. (2000). Classroom applications of cognitive theories of motivation. *Educational Psychology Review, 12,* 63–83.

U.S. Department of Education. (1999). *Twenty-first annual report to congress on the implementation of the Individuals With Disabilities Act.* Washington, DC: Author.

U.S. Department of Health and Human Services. (1999). *Mental health: A report of the surgeon general.* Rockville, MD: Author. (National Institutes of Health, National Institute of Mental Health, Substance Abuse and Mental Health Services Administration, Center for Mental Health Services).

U.S. Department of Education. (2002). *Exemplary and promising safe, disciplined and drugfree schools programs, 2001: A report of the expert panel.* Retrieved November 28, 2003, from *www.ed.gov/adminis/lead/safety/exemplary01/index.html*

Vadasy, P. F., Jenkins, J. R., Antil, L. R., Phillips, N. B., & Pool, K. (1997). The research-to-practice ball game: Classwide peer tutoring and teacher interest, implementation, and modifications. *Remedial and Special Education, 18,* 143–156.

van IJzendoorn, M. H., & de Ruiter, C. (1993). Some speculations about attachment in the schools. *International Journal of Educational Research, 19,* 597–600.

Von Brock, M. B. & Elliott, S. N. (1987). Influence of treatment effectiveness information on the acceptability of classroom interventions. *Journal of School Psychology, 25,* 131–144.

Walberg, H. (1984). Families as partners in educational productivity. *Phi Delta Kappan, 65,* 397–400.

Walker, H. M. (1995). *The acting out child: Coping with classroom disruption.* Longmont, CO: Sopris West.

Walter, J. L., & Peller, J. E. (1992). *Becoming solution-focused in brief therapy.* New York: Brunner/Mazel.

Wehmeyer, M. L., & Metzler, C. A. (1995). How self-determined are people with mental retardation?: The National Consumer Survey. *Mental Retardation, 33,* 111–119.

Weisz, J. R. (1998). Effects of interventions for child and adolescent psychological dysfunction: Relevance of context, developmental factors and individual differences. In S. Luthar, J. Burack, D. Cicchette, & J. Weisa (Eds.), *Developmental psychopathology: Perspectives on adjustment, risk and disorder* (pp. 3–22). New York: Cambridge University Press.

Wentzel, K. R. (1991a). Relations between social competence and academic achievement in early adolescence. *Child Development, 62,* 1066–1078.

Wentzel, K. R. (1991b). Social competence at school: The relation between social responsibility and academic achievement. *Review of Educational Research, 61,* 1–24.

Wentzel. K. R. (1993). Does being good make the grade?: Social behavior and academic competence in middle school. *Journal of Educational Psychology* 85(2), 357–364.

Wentzel, K. R. (1997). Student motivation in middle school: The role of perceived pedagogical caring. *Journal of Educational Psychology, 89,* 411–419.

Wentzel, K. R. (1999). Social-motivational processes and interpersonal relationships implications for understanding motivation at school. *Journal of Educational Psychology, 91,* 76–97.

Wentzel, K. R., & Watkins, D. E. (2002). Peer relationships and collaborative learning as contexts for academic enablers. *School Psychology Review, 31,* 366–377.

Werner, E. E., & Smith, R. S. (1982). *Vulnerable but invincible: A longitudinal study of resilient children and youth.* New York: Adams, Bannister, Cox.

Werner, E. E., & Smith, R. S. (1992). *Overcoming the odds: High-risk children from birth to adulthood.* Ithaca, NY: Cornell University Press.

Wilson, D. B., Gottfredson, D. C., & Najaka, S. S. (2001). School-based prevention of problem behaviors: A meta-analysis. *Journal of Quantitative Criminology, 17,* 247–272.

Witt, J., LaFleur, L., Naquin, G., & Gilbertson, D. (1999). *Teaching effective classroom routines.* Longmont, CO: Sopris West.

Wolters, C. A., & Pintrich, P. R. (1998). Contextual differences in student motivation and self-regulated learning in mathematics, English, and social studies classrooms. *Instructional Science, 26,* 27–47.

Zimmerman, B. J. (1994). Dimensions of academic self-regulation: A conceptual framework for education. In D. H. Schunk & B. J. Zimmerman (Eds.), *Self-regulation of learning and performance: Issues and educational applications.* Hillsdale, NJ: Erlbaum.

Zimmerman, B. J., Bandura, A., & Martinez-Pons, M. (1992). Self-motivation for academic attainment: The role of self-efficacy beliefs and personal goal setting. *American Educational Research Journal, 29,* 663–676.

Zimmerman, B. J., Bonner, S., & Kovach, R. (1996). *Developing self-regulated learners: Beyond achievement to self-efficacy.* Washington, DC: American Psychological Association.

Zucker, S., Brehm, K., & Doll, B. (2000, April). *ClassMaps: Making mentally healthy classrooms promotes academic success.* Paper presented at the annual meeting of the National Association of School Psychologists, New Orleans, LA.

Index

M

N

O

P

R